Cyber Minds

Insights on cybersecurity across the cloud, data, artificial intelligence, blockchain, and IoT to keep you cyber safe

Shira Rubinoff

BIRMINGHAM - MUMBAI

Cyber Minds

Acquisition Editor: Andrew Waldron
Acquisition Editor - Peer Reviews: Suresh Jain
Content Development Editor: Alex Patterson
Technical Editor: Aniket Shetty
Project Editor: Tom Jacob
Proofreader: Safis Editing
Indexer: Pratik Shirodkar
Presentation Designer: Sandip Tadge

First published: January 2020

Production reference: 1080120

Published by Packt Publishing Ltd.
Livery Place
35 Livery Street
Birmingham B3 2PB, UK.

ISBN 978-1-78980-700-4

www.packt.com

Packt>

packt.com

Subscribe to our online digital library for full access to over 7,000 books and videos, as well as industry leading tools to help you plan your personal development and advance your career. For more information, please visit our website.

Why subscribe?

- Spend less time learning and more time coding with practical eBooks and Videos from over 4,000 industry professionals
- Learn better with Skill Plans built especially for you
- Get a free eBook or video every month
- Fully searchable for easy access to vital information
- Copy and paste, print, and bookmark content

Did you know that Packt offers eBook versions of every book published, with PDF and ePub files available? You can upgrade to the eBook version at www.Packt.com and as a print book customer, you are entitled to a discount on the eBook copy. Get in touch with us at customercare@packtpub.com for more details.

At www.Packt.com, you can also read a collection of free technical articles, sign up for a range of free newsletters, and receive exclusive discounts and offers on Packt books and eBooks.

Contributors

About the author

Shira Rubinoff is a recognized cybersecurity executive, cybersecurity and blockchain advisor, global keynote speaker, and influencer who has built two cybersecurity product companies and led multiple women-in-technology efforts. She currently serves as President of the NYC-based technology incubator Prime Tech Partners and the social-media-security firm SecureMySocial. She also serves on the boards of the Executive Women's Forum for Information Security, Leading Women in Technology, the blockchain company Mainframe and the **artificial intelligence (AI)** companies TrueConnect and Pypestream.

An expert in the human factors of information technology and security, Ms. Rubinoff was named one of New Jersey's Best 50 Women in Business, was named by CSO Magazine as a Woman of Influence, was honored by CSO and the EWF with their "One to Watch" award, and was honored as the 2017 "Outstanding Woman in Infosec" by the CyberHub Summit. She has also been calculated by analysts to be the top female cybersecurity influencer globally on social media. Ms. Rubinoff also created numerous video series, including a series of interviews with the top executives of the most prominent cybersecurity and technology companies. She has published many articles, and lectures, on topics related to the human factors of cybersecurity, blockchain, and related topics, and holds several patents/patents-pending in areas related to the application of psychology to improve information technology and cybersecurity.

About the reviewer

Peter Cohen has a wealth of experience in helping organizations defend against targeted cyber-attacks—particularly those facing a legitimate threat from a nation state. His research into the long-term impact of cyber-events has been presented globally.

Peter is the EMEA Managing Director at HolistiCyber, a specialist cyber defense consultancy.

Table of Contents

Preface v

Chapter 1: Integrating Humans and Technology – Four Steps to Cyber Hygiene 1

Humans are the problem and the solution. 2

Four essential steps to achieve proper cyber hygiene. 5

Looking beyond the four steps – risky behaviors that you need to recognize 26

Chapter 2: How Risky Behavior Leads to Data Breaches. 29

Oblivious behaviors. 30

Negligent behaviors 33

Social media. 37

Takeaway – practicing cyber mindfulness 42

Looking forward – breaking down cybersecurity through interviews. . .42

Chapter 3: Blockchain – The Unwritten Chapter on Cybersecurity 45

Guenther Dobrauz-Saldapenna 47

Sally Eaves. 55

Discussion 65

Summary 69

Chapter 4: Cybersecurity in the Cloud – What You Need to Know . . . 71
Kevin L. Jackson . . . 73
Jim Reavis . . . 78
Discussion . . . 85
Summary . . . 87
Chapter 5: The World's Biggest Data Breaches – Proactive and Reactive Approaches . . . 89
Tom Kellermann . . . 91
Mary Ann Davidson . . . 100
Discussion . . . 107
Looking ahead . . . 114
Chapter 6: Trends in Cybersecurity . . . 115
Barmak Meftah . . . 117
Cleve Adams . . . 126
Discussion . . . 139
Summary . . . 143
Chapter 7: Staying Cybersecure in the IoT Revolution . . . 145
Barbara Humpton . . . 147
Ann Johnson . . . 156
Discussion . . . 165
Summary . . . 169
Chapter 8: Cyberwars – Bringing Military Lessons to Modern Information Security . . . 171
Brigadier General Gregory Touhill . . . 173
Discussion . . . 188
Summary . . . 191

Chapter 9: Can Artificial Intelligence (AI) be Trusted to Run Cybersecurity? 193
Mark Lynd 196
Joseph Steinberg 203
Discussion 214
Takeaways 218
Chapter 10: Conclusion 221
Continuous training 222
Culture of awareness 222
Up-to-date security 223
Zero Trust 223
Conclusion 224
Other Books You May Enjoy 227
Index 231

Preface

This book is inspired by my career journey, in which I've advised countless startups and have repeatedly witnessed remarkably similar cyber security challenges across a multitude of organizations. Given my educational background in psychology, I've always approached technology and cybersecurity from a vantage point that seeks to decipher the interplay of human factors with rapid technological advancement. That's why I've dedicated this book to outlining why humans are at the front and center of many problems, and in turn many solutions, in cybersecurity.

Human factors remain the key issue in cybersecurity around the world. Amidst an increasingly complex landscape, cybersecurity has always boiled down to the people, the process and the technology—three elements that must work together to maintain a cybersecure environment. Implementing technology to buttress your proactive and reactive posture will always be inadequate, unless the human element within an organization is addressed as well. In the end, the ultimate determinant of success in cybersecurity is implementing the right process, which is the bridge between people and technology.

This work is a comprehensive human-centric treatise that seeks to impart the professional lessons I've learned. These lessons are meant for business leaders to take back to their own organizations, as they confront their most profound cybersecurity challenges. This book is especially relevant to those in the C-suite who want to see a cohesive and realistic strategy, designed for humans, that can be deployed to create the conditions that foster proper cyber hygiene.

By unpackaging the human factors piece, you will be able to take a better overview of cyber hygiene and view it holistically and globally. My book provides a window into how to identify the pitfalls you may face as you work to strengthen your organization's cyber posture. Interviews with some of the top minds in the industry, coupled with my commentary, provide further insights, real-world examples, and lessons that are applicable and actionable to quell some of the most formidable cyber challenges I've seen throughout my professional journey.

I sincerely hope you enjoy the book, and look to it as a resource for you and your organization.

Dedication

This book is dedicated to my daughters:

PENINA, MIMI & TAMMY

My girls... you inspire me every day. Three sisters who are so different, yet so similar.

You all possess hearts of gold, love and compassion for others, and who are never afraid of rolling up their sleeves and jumping right in when an opportunity arises.

I am so proud to be your mother and will always support your dreams and goals in life. No dream is too big, no goal too lofty.

Always remember, in life, you always have choices – the first should be – how you face it – face life from a positive angle, happiness can be a choice too.

I am looking forward to continually being inspired by you and I am always incredibly proud of my three girls...

1

Integrating Humans and Technology – Four Steps to Cyber Hygiene

This book is about humans, the interaction between people and technology, and the process that surrounds that constant interaction. Throughout the book, you'll notice that technical and organizational dynamics are often discussed together. That's because it's hard to separate the two; humans are at the front and center of every cybersecurity decision and action you take.

While human factors are not the be all and end all in achieving a secure organization, they certainly play a crucial role in every organization's security measures. You have to talk about cybersecurity from a macro view that's inclusive of the human factors at every step of the way. Every organization needs, in my experience, to take four essential steps to build a culture of effective and meaningful cyber hygiene, and bind the human and technical foundations of cybersecurity together: continuous training, global awareness, regular updates, and Zero Trust. Cybersecurity doesn't exist in a vacuum, and effective guidance of your organization's cyber hygiene needs to take into account the cultural realities that make up your organization's environment.

To deliver the critical information needed to fully comprehend cybersecurity, I thought a lot about the people having a profound impact on our industry and the focus they could provide through their insight.

I engaged them, and through dialogue, interviews, and then subsequent takeaways that I present, I approached future concerns and corresponding solutions, and the overlap they have with the real-world challenges occurring as we speak.

After we fully examine the role of humans at every level of cybersecurity, we'll review how cybersecurity intersects with the following areas through wide-reaching conversations about blockchain technology, the cloud, proactive and reactive approaches to data breaches, the **Internet of Things (IoT)**, augmented reality, and artificial intelligence.

Humans are the problem and the solution

Human factors and cybersecurity go hand-in-hand. First, to be cyber-secure, the elements of security technology must be addressed. While you're executing this monumental task, remember that human factors ought to be a fundamental consideration when creating your security protocols. How humans are approached when implementing security compliance will ultimately determine the level of security within a given organization.

The human is the weakest link in the cybersecurity chain; make them part of the solution, not the problem.

In my experience, this is the most powerful sentence to consider when thinking about the overall cybersecurity of an organization. I repeat, the human is always the weakest link in the security chain; and that's true on both sides of security. Security is built to protect humans, but it's built by humans and the bad actors attempting to break down security are human too. Humans are the common thread, always the centerpiece of both the security problem and the solution.

Given that there are humans involved in every step of the way, an organization can decide to take the view that humans are the problem and govern from that perspective. Alternatively, they can flip their vantage point and take the position that humans are the solution.

With that in mind, they can implement proper cyber hygiene in the organization, while simultaneously unifying their team, as humans take center-stage as the solution. Needless to say, the latter is a much more compelling and effective way to tackle your greatest security challenges.

Making humans the linchpin of your organization's security solutions empowers your employees. It also helps to lay the groundwork for a loyal and cohesive workforce, bound together and working in concert, ensuring your company is secure from the inside out.

Following this philosophy, you'll be much more likely to create an environment with proper cyber hygiene, which is crucial in today's ever-more-dangerous world. Cyber hygiene is pivotal in curtailing both malicious insider threats from disgruntled or opportunistic employees, and non-malicious insider threats from oblivious or negligent employees.

Organizational culture is the tie that binds people together, and that inevitably determines the efficacy of entire organizations. It's important to step back and review how the culture around cybersecurity has evolved substantially in recent times, and how it's become an entirely different process over the years.

Compliance culture versus security culture

Compliance culture was the norm for many years, adopted across countless organizations to promote cyber safety. That world is now long gone. Security culture is now the standard model that many organizations have embraced as a practical necessity for proper organizational cyber hygiene.

Compliance culture – top-down mandate

It's not rocket science: Compliance culture was exactly like it sounds. Be compliant!

If you take a peek at the definition in the Merriam-Webster Dictionary, you'll see that compliance is "the act or process of complying with a desire, demand proposal, or regimen."

Accordingly, you can probably already guess how an organization's compliance culture played out nearly everywhere. The rule set was established by the top of the organization, with the goal of complying with the relevant legislation at minimal cost, and implemented all the way down through every level of an organization. This was a one-size-fits-all model that harkened back to the command-and-control style of management that was prevalent in the 20th century.

Rules were made at the top and no-one else had any input whatsoever. This top-down rulemaking would percolate through all facets of the organization with little to no feedback from its employees. This was an iron fist model of "you do as the checklist says or else." Deviating from established processes, or going beyond the regulatory requirements, was frowned upon if not outright forbidden. Being a good "citizen" of a compliance culture meant not rocking the boat and staying in your lane.

Security culture – a secure environment

The security model approach is different in almost every way. The perception of security shifts and becomes geared toward a collective approach, with the goal of ensuring that the company remains secure. There's an understanding that legislation is just a starting point and the cost of an insecure system is far greater than the cost of good security. This philosophical foundation makes it widely understood that security is everyone's responsibility, and teamwork is an essential part of that process.

This seismic shift doesn't mean that compliance and jobs specifically focused on cybersecurity are replaced. Instead, their roles become better integrated with the rest of the organization. Seamless dialogue and collaboration are relentlessly encouraged to help bolster security measures. While protocol remains in place, it's tailored appropriately to the employees as humans who share collective responsibility for cybersecurity. Job descriptions don't absolve anyone of their individual responsibility to contribute to cybersecurity organization-wide.

Now that we've learned about how leveraging the human aspects of security is critical to ensuring success, and how security culture is the new norm, let's move on to the four steps I consider essential for instituting proper cyber hygiene.

Continuous training is the first building block in this process, as it gives new security measures a better chance of being embraced by your employees.

Four essential steps to achieve proper cyber hygiene

In today's world, your company's integrity hinges on protecting your data, and by extension your customer's data. That's why proper cyber hygiene is imperative. To execute this task, there are four steps to deal with both technological considerations and human factors that you should follow, to implement proper cyber hygiene and keep your organization secure:

1. Continuous training for all employees – from janitor to intern, to consultant to CEO, no matter what job they have in the organization, all employees need to be included.
2. Promoting a culture of global awareness throughout the organization.
3. Updated security and patching on a regular basis.
4. Implementing a stringent Zero Trust model.

Before we delve into the mechanics of the four steps in the implementation of cyber hygiene in your organization, I want you to fully understand the pivotal nature of human factors in any cybersecurity framework.

The human factors in proper cyber hygiene

The reason we're starting with the human factors, instead of the technological ones, is that if the human factors are not accounted for then all the security technology you might use is completely wasted.

It's convenient to ignore or bypass awkward or extended security, and if the people in your organization don't understand why the security protocols in place are necessary, then convenience will win out every time. In that case, even the most up-to-date security measures are wasted.

On the other hand, an engaged and informed workforce is a massive boost to any security endeavor, bringing the combined intelligence of your employees to bear on the problem of security and hunting down overlooked gaps in your defenses. Engaged people are the foundation of cybersecurity, so it's essential that we start by discussing how to engage them.

Step 1 – Continuous training for all employees

Training has to be open-ended, multifaceted, and varied in its methods to convey understanding and spark swift adaptation. Having multiple methods of continuous training empowers your employees to choose the option that suits them best.

Multiple methods are also critically important from both a morale perspective and a legal perspective. In terms of morale, the employee will feel more comfortable following their choice of training method and more satisfied by charting their own course. Legally, if the organization imposes a certain way of training for all employees, accusations of bias may arise where a person feels like they haven't been included.

In the end, the journey may be different for each and every person within an organization, but the end result will be the same. You're going to want to keep it relevant, interesting, and meaningful. I can't stress enough that appropriateness is everything when it comes to training, and a critical part of this step is knowing your audience.

We need to lean on our understanding of human psychology, and how different cohorts, typically segmented by age, view the world. Age-specific messaging has cascading effects for a person within an organization, and can help them understand why these practices need to become an immediate part of their habits to solidify your organization's cyber hygiene.

Know your audience for training – communicating with different generational cohorts

We live in a transitional age, where the cross-generational employee population is more common than ever. That's why when we look at continuous training, we have to consider the demography and lens through which different generations view the world.

This is a good training practice for any new information, but I've found that it's especially important in cybersecurity.

We find ourselves at an inflection point in the workplace, as this is the first time in history where we have at least four generations working side by side – Baby Boomers, Gen X, Millennials, and Gen Z, all with different views on life, work-life balance, problem solving, communication, learning, and social sharing. Each generation has grown up in a very different world when it comes to the usage of technology and how it interplayed with their lives. Their stances on privacy, sharing or oversharing information, how best to work, and how to maintain a good work-life balance all differ from each other.

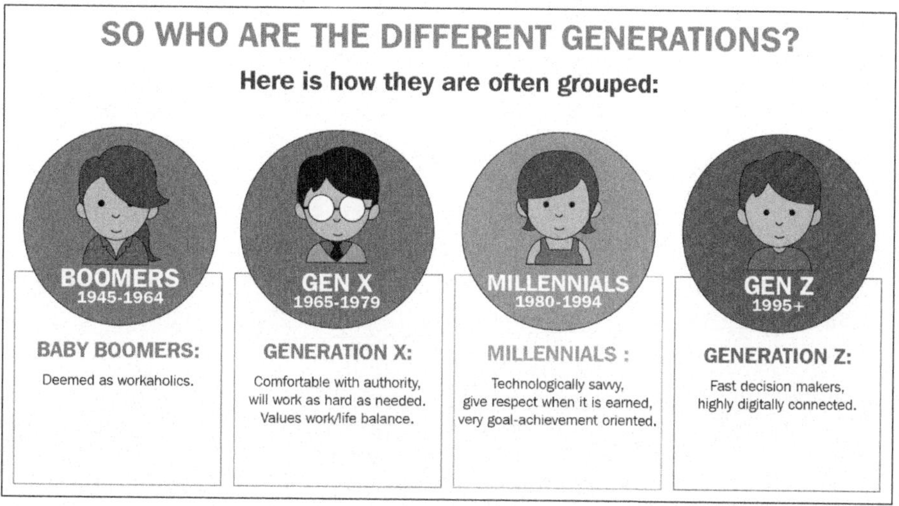

Communication is key for effective leadership within an organization, so by extension it's important to know your audience when you're training. Part of that is keeping aware of how each generational cohort processes information and instruction differently. As you train different folks within your organization and steer them toward your cyber goals, you'll discover that their different styles inevitably influence their workflow.

Some of these differences are readily apparent if you regularly interact with different generational cohorts. Boomers value face-to-face interaction, old-fashioned phone calls, and long-form conversations that convey, in full detail, the important message and all the other pertinent information that they need to know.

Any other form of communication might be considered impersonal, if not rude, to this generation that values human interaction more than their successors.

Jumping over to the other end of the age groups, Millennials and Gen Z often scoff at phone calls or in-person meetings, especially if the information could have been transferred by some form of messaging. In fact, most younger people are jarred by phone calls, don't use landline phones, and have the ringer on their cell phones on silent most of the time.

These stereotypes don't always hold up, but they're a good starting point. Gen X are especially mixed, and depending on their personality and work style, can embody a mix of several generations' communication style. These are starting points, and if you find they don't hold true for an individual, then your approach needs to change to take that into account.

New ways of training versus old ways of training

The era of annual training events is over. In the past, companies would hold a one-day event either once a year (or in the best case once a quarter) where employees would be taught, lectured, and made aware of security measures. The training would also speed through attacks that the employees should be aware of, a litany of compliance regulations, and relevant protocol that would be put in place.

These events were big splashes where engaging speakers were brought in, hands-on activities were conducted, cutting edge videos were shown, catered lunches and snacks were served, and even maybe a bit of entertainment was provided to take the edge off. These full day fetes were viewed as "home runs" because they captured the employee's undivided attention, with the expectation that they would remember, in full detail, what went on that day and fully comply with every single detail that was shared in this one-stop training.

You've probably gathered why we've moved far beyond this approach. We are human, and we don't remember things well unless we remind ourselves of them often. Unless a person has continuous training around security, they will likely remember snippets or barely anything at all.

When a business has continuous training in place, it remains "top of mind" for the employees. As the training is reinforced it will become second nature, part of the background culture of the organization.

Cybersecurity is ever-changing, so it's only reasonable to conclude that frequent training is needed; but that training should be continuous, rather than staccato, and woven into ordinary workflows instead of seeming like an occasional drip of new responsibilities.

Information dumps versus incremental training

Training for cyber hygiene is complex and extensive. It's a lot to digest all at once. That's precisely why continuous training must reject the old way of doing things, where informational dumps would unload what your employees needed to know to do their job properly.

In my experience, information dumps lead to information overload in just the same way as antiquated annual training. Companies used to, and sometimes still do, overload their employees with everything they need to know about security, compliance, and protocol all at once – along with every possible scenario that might arise, all in one mighty lump of information. It often went with an even bigger handbook, and a phrase like "Here you go, employee, study this so you know it all, and every possible scenario that may come from it. Do not forget anything because everything is important." Clearly, this method sets nearly everyone up for failure.

I've found, and I'm sure you have too, that no employee is able to digest information of that magnitude and fully integrate the new material into their routine overnight. We can't fight nature, and that's why incremental training makes more sense; both from a time perspective and when taking into account the limits of the human ability to consume information.

Schedule training accordingly, and break it down into categories. Make each category meaningful in its own right, with relevant scenarios to explain the importance of the information you're sharing. In the end, that gives your employees a much greater chance of retaining essential information.

Universally applicable versus situationally relevant

Be vigilant in avoiding the fallacy that anything is universally applicable, and that training sessions can be universal as a result. Just because one person wholeheartedly believes that they've identified the best way to train employees, in a very cost- and time-effective way that trains many groups all at once, doesn't mean they're correct.

Picture a universal training session: a huge room with a thousand people in it, all from different disciplines, markets, and sectors. Up at the podium stands a speaker poised to give a very important talk about privacy, security, compliance, and real-world scenarios. The speaker begins to speak, delivering a broad-ranging conversation to cover a hodgepodge of dissimilar sectors, such as healthcare, finance, insurance, government, and every other industry.

Next, she spits out an alphabet soup of regulations with which the audience may or may not be familiar: HIPAA, SEC, EPA, and so on. Undoubtedly, there are scores of people that are already completely lost, or at best encountering content that they're woefully unfamiliar with, because it's far beyond their background. That universal training session has instead become an information nightmare that's going to be anything but effective.

In stark contrast to universal training is situationally relevant training. If you have a room full of people from the same background or industry, dealing with similar issues, regulations, and compliance concerns, you can deliver laser-focused training for that specific demographic. For example, the financial industry will have very specific compliance concerns that differ from healthcare: pension regulations, financial privacy laws, and a very different public perception of the industry to name a few.

You can keep attention and focus on these people's specific sector, discussing relevant information pertaining just to them. Privacy, compliance, and regulations can all be seamlessly covered to inspire meaning and lay the stakes for acquiring habits.

A very broad setting is a recipe for one to tune out from the get-go. It's important to get and keep the attention of someone you're training; their ability to find themselves in the stories you tell and find real relevance in the discussions that follow will build their capacity to achieve proper cyber hygiene.

Stage real-life scenarios

Security shouldn't just be a concept that is discussed, but a reality that is lived. That's why, for training purposes, simulating real-life scenarios can be greatly influential. Walk your team through what they should do when problems arise by using these simulations. Afterward, have the team dissect and discuss what went wrong as a group, and how "we" could have improved the outcome or the end result.

Stress the "we," as in "we are a group that supports each other through these critical moments." It may sound trite, but remember that working as a team is infinitely stronger than working alone.

Think about human physiology. If you make a fist without using your thumb, it has no strength. Just like the strength is in the hand as a whole, we are only as strong as our weakest link, and that weakest link can be any employee from any level within the organization.

Everyone has to be supported, and it's imperative that every team member operates as an integral and indispensable part of a collective unit. This lays the foundation for a globally aware culture, which is Step 2 in your quest toward achieving meaningful cyber hygiene.

Step 2 – Global awareness and culture for cyber hygiene

In an age of unprecedented interconnectivity and globalization, your organization has to reflect today's realities. We're in a competitive labor market, and getting and keeping quality talent is a constant challenge. It's sad but true: millions of jobs are left open because of the dearth of relevant skills among today's workforce, and this is especially the case in the field of cybersecurity.

Today's big corporate players prioritize company culture and promote purpose as a matter of necessity. These things were previously thought of as squishy and hard to define, but now they're recognized as more pivotal than ever to modern employees. Belonging and overall workplace satisfaction are essential components in any company's effectiveness and competitiveness.

We can look to any part of our lives, and wherever we feel appreciated, valued and heard we naturally feel more aligned, loyal and productive in that environment. By natural extension, we'll practice better cyber hygiene, too.

A globally aware culture that promotes cyber hygiene does so by promoting a positive environment, where constant dialogue and unfettered collaboration are key indicators of organizational health. As mentioned earlier, employees are seen as part of the solution instead of the problem, and are made aware of changes that are needed via relevant flows of communication.

It's very easy to point fingers at someone and call them the problem, rather than dig for the root cause of risky or unsafe behavior. Empower your employees to be part of the solution. Continuous training and awareness will keep the protocols fresh, and their minds sharp, but it's also essential in my experience to gather feedback and let information flow both ways.

In our cut-throat world, it's of utmost importance that your employees feel supported by the management team. They need to be aware that if they report a potential problem or misaligned behavior, it will be welcomed, not frowned upon for possibly "blowing a false whistle." The worst-case mindset for your employees is that if they stay quiet, and just do as they're told, they can't be held responsible for a problem. More often than not, this is the current case in most organizations when it comes to speaking up or reporting a problem.

I've found that transparency is the best sanitizer. Transparency is a key ingredient in a globally aware organization to preserve a stellar work environment for their employees. If you encourage feedback, and allow your employees to question what has been implemented, you may discover you haven't been asking the right questions. This new way of looking at things may uncover a faulty part of your security, which when fixed will strengthen your defenses throughout the organization. Your employees may have "eyes and ears" in areas that you may not be focused on – encouraging their feedback will likely help you find areas that need strengthening in your organization. Utilizing this most valuable resource, your employee, benefits you from a morale and security standpoint.

Building an inclusive workforce – diversity is at the heart of global awareness

When we think about diversity, we often hone in on obvious demographic indicators such as gender, age, culture, demographic, and socio-economic status. These are definitely important and should not be trivialized, but as a globally aware organization, you should frame diversity differently. For companies, demographic diversity boils down to diversity of thought, approach, and viewpoints. Diversity means having employees who view the world quite differently from one another because of the lenses of their background, upbringing, education, and a multitude of other factors that have shaped and molded them.

Think about a phenomenon we see far too often: A company entirely made up of people of a similar gender, age group, culture, race, demographic, or socio-economic status. This situation almost never improves organically, because recruiting through existing employees' social networks at monolithic organizations tends to reinforce this demographic disaster.

Without diversity, any organization will consistently yield remarkably narrow and irrelevant conclusions and attack problems in a very limited way, especially in their approach to security and privacy. How could it not? A monoculture is scientifically vulnerable to disease because of its lack of genetic diversity. Similarly, creating an echo chamber within organizations through limited demographic diversity leads to suboptimal outcomes, including woefully inadequate security.

The pitfalls of a demographic monoculture

Let's walk through two scenarios to better illustrate the difference between diverse and globally aware organizations, and those that are painfully stuck in the past.

For the first scenario, picture a group of 10 employees, all 40- and 50-year-old Caucasian men, all of whom have attended top Ivy League schools and come with strong business and finance experience. They all have their MBA, were raised in upper-middle- or upper-class households, played sports in college, are married with two to three kids, and have similar religious beliefs.

Before any serious business dialogue even begins, they have a chance to socialize for a little while, and quickly discover the immense number of similarities they have in common. Differences will be cast aside, and these jaw-dropping similarities are going to create a warm feeling of comfort and belonging in the room. Dissention and discomfort will be non-existent in this remarkably cookie-cutter crowd.

Imagine that this group is then presented with a topic to problem-solve. One person is appointed to lead the discussion, and to encourage collaboration, communication, and feedback. He gets up and starts the ball rolling, with the new colleagues to whom he has already bonded.

The die has been cast for this monoculture of men, and each one of them will behave as if they "belong to a club." In effect, they will create an echo chamber in which if one person makes his position clear, there will be little to no dissention from his other colleagues. As the building blocks of an idea are laid out, complete collaboration will take hold, with few alternatives.

Welcome to the world of a monoculture of people and ideas. As ideas are thrown out into the discussion, the nods and words of encouragement and agreement are seen and heard. If one disagrees, the nature of that group will lend itself to words like, "We're all on the same page." Rarely will someone rock the boat and propose a competing idea in such a bonded group of like-minded men.

Now, consider scenario two: Envision a room with 10 people that's teeming with diversity. This group is gender-balanced, from a breadth of cultures, a variety of socio-economic backgrounds, and a wide range of beliefs. This cohort is also racially and ethnically diverse, bringing together a plethora of educational backgrounds, personal hobbies, and career journeys.

It's the first scenario turned on its head, as the people in the room rapidly discover the immense number of differences they have with each other. Inevitably, those differences will be highlighted and even embraced, creating an inquisitive buzz and interest in the room.

If this diverse set of folks is presented with the same problem as the previous group, their radically different walks of life will encourage collaboration, communication, and especially feedback.

There's no "club" to belong to that could hold them back, and they instead get up and get the ball rolling when challenging situations arise. Because there's such a diverse group of people in the room, there will be a wealth of different positions, perspectives, viewpoints, even to the point of complete disagreement in the room at times. The richness of diversity of thought will provide entirely new ways of looking at challenges. Some viewpoints expressed or highlighted will be completely novel to other members of the group.

In my experience, between the two scenarios, there is only one option you want in your business. A diverse workplace coupled with a collaborative and communicative management approach yields diverse thoughts and solutions, and brings a wealth of information, experiences, and ideas to the table that you might never have otherwise considered.

Global awareness begins by leveraging diversity for better results. In cybersecurity, this is crucial in achieving a higher level of security within an organization. Diversity of thought and mind from wider demographics addresses challenges around security, whereas I've found homogenous groups often omit, miss, or entirely ignore them.

Communicate for a global world – advertising strategies are a good start

Communication in a global world is tricky when your ranks are teeming with diversity. That's why your communication strategy should piggy-back off of the foundational ideas in advertising. If you take a look at the advertising world, you'll see that advertisements are not a "one size fits all" model. Each advertisement is geared to its appropriate audience and demographic, to make it impactful and relatable to its target audience. Yes, creating multiple advertisements for the same object to appeal to a wide audience may be expensive, but as we've all experienced, it's needed to catch our eye. We each need to be able to attach ourselves to the object or idea in some fashion. If we can't, the advertisement will go right by us without implanting a need or connection to the item or idea. Communication without impact is basically the same as no communication at all.

To build the groundwork for sound cyber hygiene, every member of the targeted employee audience needs to feel that the message is relatable to them, talking to them, or needed by them, so that they become attached to the message in a meaningful way. We want to spur buy-in, in a similar way to how advertisers want to spur the desire to go out and buy a particular item. We want employees to accept and integrate the idea presented. This isn't a novel approach – advertisers caught on the need for personalization and relevancy a long time ago.

If, instead, we force conformity and order people to defy their natural instincts, we'll produce massive frustration instead. The toxicity of that frustration can lead to employees experiencing the feeling of not being valued by their organization. Going back to the problem with top-down mandates, employees begin to disengage, find themselves facing chronic dissatisfaction, and decide not to stick around in the long term, as their loyalty wanes. This creates significant issues in your organization and your cybersecurity.

We have to think critically about our communication patterns and employ a multifaceted approach to leverage the different mediums we have at our disposal. We have to cast a wide net to make our necessary protocols resonate with everyone at the organization. To get organization-wide buy-in, we have to make our ranks feel comfortable and stimulated, and familiar with what we need from them to create a cyber secure organization.

In my experience, in practice this means you're going to have to think about the employees you're targeting. Break them down into groups and segment them. Analyze how they like to learn and what they get excited about; dive deeper and examine what methods of learning might inspire higher levels of comfort and familiarity for each group. Find out what kind of messaging and delivery is appealing to each respective demographic. For example, when it comes to millennials, gamified learning or training is often a good tool; think about making that one of the methods you make available to them.

Pay attention to the details that define your employees. Take the time to get to know them, show interest in their work, and understand who they are as people. Celebrate their birthdays, and look them in the eye as you talk to them; even that one moment of full focus is meaningful.

In turn, they will feel valued, and that happy, cohesive, and loyal atmosphere will set the stage for success across your organization both from a human and a security standpoint. When people are valued and feel integrated into a larger collective, loyalty naturally follows. If you don't seek to build that connection, if people feel taken advantage of or dismissed, they could express their grievances with actions and that negativity can eventually undermine organizations.

Transitioning to technical underpinnings of proper cyber hygiene

Now that we've thoroughly reviewed the organizational dynamics that are necessary for proper cyber hygiene, we can move on to the essential technical considerations of Step 3 and Step 4. Cyber dangers remain persistent, and we must have the right technological foundations and security protocols to keep our organizations safe.

Always recall that these technologies and protocols don't exist in a vacuum. They are built, operated, and breached by humans. A human-centric approach to cybersecurity should always be at the forefront of proper cyber hygiene. If you ignore human factors, you do so at your own peril – don't expect good results without viewing everything through the lens of our shared humanity.

The rational basis for framing cyber hygiene as a human-powered endeavor is straightforward. Humans remain the weakest link in the security chain, and simultaneously the problem and the solution. Don't forget that even while I'm discussing technical specifications and protocols, human beings remain front and center of any step that solidifies good cyber hygiene.

Step 3 – Updated security and patching

To begin Step 3, let's talk about a simple concept that might seem a little obvious to some, but is in fact often overlooked by cybersecurity professionals around the world. It's common sense to keep your systems updated and patched at all times, but you would be surprised how many businesses and organizations fail to do exactly that.

It's crucial for an organization to have up-to-date security and patching throughout their environment, which inevitably means running up-to-date **operating systems (OSs)**. This can be a daunting task for big organizations that don't have a good handle on every single device they're currently operating. Nevertheless, this is something you can't ignore. If you're not running a current OS, you're already setting the stage for eventual disaster.

Think about what happens when a new patch becomes available, and you need to implement that patch throughout your organization. When you take on that monumental task, you're operating under the assumption that your OSs are the latest versions available, and are therefore supported by the manufacturer. If you're running old OSs instead, they won't be supported and no patches will be created for ongoing security issues. This is always, in my experience, a one-way ticket to cybersecurity failure. In sum, please run updated OSs at all times if you want to patch effectively, and have proper cyber hygiene overall. Period.

Averting a crisis – updating is everything

You might be wondering why there are so many high-profile cyber incidents in today's world. Even with billions of dollars spent on cybersecurity yearly, let's talk about just why successful data breaches are so common. Threats have clearly proliferated; we've seen so many Fortune 100 companies that fall victim to massive breaches that we've grown numb to them. But there's another piece to this puzzle. Looking from the outside, one would think that these companies that were breached would naturally have the latest and greatest security, with little or no possibility for a breach. Clearly this is not the case as many companies ignore their obvious security weaknesses.

For instance, you might not know that the big Equifax hack that exposed 143 million customers' personal data to unknown cybercriminals could have been entirely avoided (`https://www.cnet.com/news/equifaxs-hack-one-year-later-a-look-back-at-how-it-happened-and-whats-changed/`). It turns out that the company was using out-of-date software with a known security weakness.

You might be pondering: Why didn't Equifax, and other major corporations that fell victim to similar data breaches, stay up to date on their security and patching?

It would be reasonable to assume that they would protect themselves and their customer's data, but evidently they utterly failed in that endeavor. In my opinion, we can blame both technical and organizational dynamics trickling down from management, at that company and many, many others.

A cognizant C-suite – management that comprehends security and patching trickles down

Bringing the human factors back in, let's talk about the inextricable connection between updated security and patching and organizations that practice true cyber hygiene. A model organization would have top executives in place, schooled in the importance of having cybersecurity teams, and who work around the clock when vulnerabilities arise.

If there exist in your organization paths for attackers to breach your internal systems and access sensitive data, you're already making your bed and setting yourself up for a cyber incident where you'll have to lie in it. One effective solution is to implement the safer practice of storing that data on computers disconnected – or "air-gapped" – from the internet.

Unfortunately, when senior management and executives at companies aren't educated enough around these issues and aren't the most tech-savvy, they often lack understanding of what's at stake. More importantly, they don't know how to quickly protect the valuable information that's been entrusted to them by their company and their customers. Cognizance of what's at stake at the top of the organization ultimately determines the level of security that can be achieved organization-wide.

The need for proactive and reactive security posture

It's pivotal that the entire team, not just management, practices and promotes a security posture that's both proactive and reactive, by understanding the risks and problems that occur if and when employees create paths for an attacker.

You have to be proactive in the sense that you have to think ahead and strategically plan for threats that may be coming around the bend even before they unfold.

Additionally, you have to be reactive as you have to respond as quickly as possible to any breaches, to contain the damage. This mixed posture is an essential ingredient in cybersecurity that you'll see me return to throughout the book.

The need for a proactive and reactive security posture is making waves throughout the cybersecurity world. Today, there are many corporations that are acutely aware of the need to better integrate development and operations in a rapidly changing cyber landscape.

Proactively, **SecDevOps** (a term that refers to united **sec**urity, **dev**elopment, and **op**erations when they work together toward a common goal) marries secure development and deployment, allowing for radical simplification of security patching and updates. This is quickly becoming the new norm among many large companies, who want to strike a better balance between efficiency and security.

Reactively, there are tools such as AI that can help us figure out when something isn't behaving as expected, and swiftly kill any possibility of a breach occurring, or spinning out of control when it does.

The cost of a breach – the stakes are always high

Let's take a moment to consider the staggering cost of a data breach. The Ponemon Institute found that the global average cost of a data breach is around $3.62 million dollars, and that was back in 2017. Lately, some breaches are costing organizations many times that (`https://digitalguardian.com/blog/whats-cost-data-breach-2019`). I will note here that it's important in my experience for organizations to purchase cyber insurance. The kind of breach and amount covered by the policy will vary by organization, but I believe it is a must-have for all organizations in this day and age. It won't mitigate the damage of a breach, but it is a tool that can help soften the blow financially.

The costs of breaches tend to be much higher in the industrialized world, where regulatory fines are higher and the cost of downtime can devastate a company's bottom line. Nevertheless, wherever breaches happen, they tend to be very costly and cause reputational fallout that reverberates for years to come.

Transitioning to Zero Trust

Now that we're moving on to Step 4, you might be thinking that you can confidently approach all of the milestones that I've laid out thus far. I have news for you: if you don't have a Zero Trust model, proper cyber hygiene is always going to be a millstone around the neck of your organization.

I want to paint a clear picture of what having a Zero Trust model looks like and why you need it to fully implement proper cyber hygiene. You can have superb training, be the very archetype of a globally aware organization, and strictly adhere to best practices in updating your security and implemented necessary patching – but it could all fall apart spectacularly without having a Zero Trust model.

Step 4 – Implementing a Zero Trust model

Let's start with the basics: Zero Trust is a security theory based on the belief that organizations should not automatically give access to or trust anything inside or outside of its perimeter. The organization should instead verify everything trying to connect to its systems before granting access.

Zero Trust means, as a first step, cutting off all access. You cannot trust anyone without the proper verification that lets the network know who they are. This policy of no access whatsoever extends to machines, IP addresses, and so on, until one is a known entity and can be properly authorized.

The Zero Trust model of cybersecurity highlights the real need for proper identity management. In the past, organizations would only focus on protecting and defending their perimeter. There was a broad understanding that everyone was safe within the confines of their organization – never taking into consideration the worry of insider threats that could open them up to breaches. Therefore, if a hacker or bad actor was already inside the perimeter, further internal access was readily granted. The focus was on protecting the perimeter of the business to keep the data safe.

It was common to think that the enemy would be at the walls, trying to breach the perimeter, but the employees inside the perimeter would be perfectly safe and fine because they are employees of the organization.

Over time, cybersecurity leaders and experts highlighted many extreme data breaches and analyzed the weaknesses behind them. They found that these breaches occurred because hackers who were able to get access into the corporation were then easily able to move throughout the internal system, and gain access to the information they desired. Their access was limitless because they became trusted once they got inside the perimeter. Once they get in, they can do a lot of damage.

Zero Trust protects an organization from these types of attacks, as identity is key not only for safeguarding the perimeter of the organization, but also internally. A lockdown on information is instituted, where access is only granted to the data if the proper identity protocol is followed each and every time the data is accessed. It's no longer the case that if you have access to one area, you've been handed the keys to the kingdom. That's why carrying out a Zero Trust policy is a critical piece of the puzzle in your quest to achieve proper cyber hygiene.

Zero Trust, insider threats, and attacks

Understanding and combating insider threats and attacks go hand-in-hand with implementing proper cyber hygiene. This is a part of the security culture that needs to be embraced by your organization. Streamlining your security across your organization is critical. Effective teamwork in this area is about cohesiveness, respect from management to your employees and from them to their management.

When new security protocols are being implemented into your organization, explain to your employees why they're needed and consistently make them part of the solution. Employees need to feel valued, heard, and supported by their management. A security culture that's felt and lived by all in the organization will cut the numbers of insider threats by leaps and bounds, if done correctly. To really put this plan into motion, however, you need to understand the different kinds of insider threats.

Malicious and non-malicious insider threats/attacks

There are two different types of insider threats or attacks. Malicious attacks are perpetrated by either an opportunistic employee, or a disgruntled employee.

Malicious attacks are identified (by Shaw 2005) as follows:

Opportunistic employees:

- Are motivated by their personal, selfish desires around money or opportunity
- Can be any gender
- Have access across the organization, which could be physical, digital, or both
- Have the ability to rationalize the illicit act (moral rationalization)
- Highly technically skilled
- Suffered a recent (past 6 months) adverse event, at work or in their personal life

The best way to combat the threat of opportunistic employees is as follows:

- Position rotation and cross-training
- Mandatory vacation policies
- Regular audits
- Visible monitoring
- Transparent and rapid sanctions

Disgruntled employees:

- Are motivated by ego
- Are more likely to be male
- Are the "lord of their fiefdom," exerting great personal control over their sphere of work
- Have an overblown sense of entitlement
- Display a history of negative social and personal behaviors, often requiring intervention from management
- Have a lack of social skills, or exhibit strong social isolation
- Were part of a recent inciting incident, in which they lost face or power, which they consider an embarrassment

Combat disgruntled employees as follows:

- Firm controls on who can and cannot access different areas of business
- Clear role boundaries that limit responsibility creep
- Cross-functional teams
- Management training to recognize problematic behavioral changes
- Robust and automatic post-termination protocols to remove access from terminated employees

A Zero Trust model covers many of the necessary protocols to protect from a malicious insider threat. As an important component of proper cyber hygiene, this kind of threat can be minimized or even eliminated.

A non-malicious insider threat can manifest itself in a number of ways, the first being the oblivious employee – one who is oblivious to security protocols and security awareness in the organization. We cover the risky behavior and common mistakes these insider threats can make extensively in *Chapter 2*, *How Risky Behavior Leads to Data Breaches*, and discuss several methods your company can put into place to mitigate these risks.

This brings us back to continuous training and global awareness in an organization – keeping security and cyber hygiene at the forefront of your employees' minds. Always make your employees feel supported by their management team. Uncertainty yields a lack of decisiveness, which then leads to mistakes or sloppiness around security. When an employee feels supported by their management, they're more likely to go to them with a question or problem, and take proper action when the need arises.

The dangers of social engineering

Another important identifying type of non-malicious insider threat is an employee who can be easily socially engineered. You may think that it's hard to do, especially to a senior executive in an organization.

Imagine a criminal, Xander, wants to gain access to a secure part of a building where credentials and identity are taken very seriously. Xander does not have the proper identity or credentials. If Xander still tries to gain access, even though he does not have the proper credentials, he will be refused entry. The system works, right?

Imagine another criminal, Yvette, also attempting to gain access to the same environment without proper identity or credentials. Yvette, however, understands that social engineering may be her way in, by preying on the weakest link in the security chain – the human. Yvette did her homework and found out that someone in that secure environment they want to gain access to is very pregnant. Yvette approaches the secure environment with bags of baby presents looped on both arms, carrying a huge cake for the "surprise baby shower" that someone in the office is supposedly throwing for their pregnant colleague. Doors fly open; people even hold doors for Yvette that typically need specialized card access. How can this happen in a secure environment where credentials are needed for access, but aren't present upon entry?

In this case, access was granted because of a well-played social engineering technique. It's simple to identify baby gifts and a huge cake as a celebration. This is something most people are fond of and like to be part of when they can. Since the employees know they have a pregnant colleague, there was no question in their minds about whether this celebration was indeed truly happening. The physical components of this celebration were present, so their minds file Yvette away as "allowed," since she fits the profile of someone belonging to a celebration that it makes sense to be occurring.

Yvette was smart enough to be laden down with gifts and a big cake – thus utilizing another social engineering technique, of hoping for a "good Samaritan" to hold the door, being distracted by the gifts and cake and not requesting the proper credentials for entry, since Yvette's hands were occupied. A bystander watching this exchange would rationalize that Yvette was "allowed" to be here, because why else would she be carrying presents and a cake? I'm a good citizen and want to be part of this celebration, and that cake looks soooo good.

Social engineering appeals to human behaviors by making someone believe an action or circumstance is taking place by utilizing an element, props, distractions, tricking techniques, or bogus credentials to help someone believe that what they are seeing or hearing is true.

Zero Trust in this case would also help protect the organization, with access only allowed with proper credentials, both technical and physical. A cake and presents aren't proper credentials for access. Pausing, and not getting caught up in a situation, but focusing on real, known technical and physical credentials will curtail social engineering techniques from putting your employees and organization at risk.

Slow down the situation and have protocols in place, to educate your employees and protect them from social engineering. When it comes to non-malicious assistance to malicious attacks, your employees aren't actively trying to hurt the organization; often times, they're unaware and ill-trained in ways to help protect themselves and the organization.

Looking beyond the four steps – risky behaviors that you need to recognize

In this opening chapter, we looked at what I consider the four vital steps to solidify your cyber hygiene, and how to implement these steps across all facets of your organization. In the next chapter, we'll look at examples of how certain employee behaviors are outsized drivers of risk and how to mitigate or quash those patterns.

As a clear takeaway, you should have a substantial grasp of what's at stake and what it takes to practice proper hygiene in today's world. Humans are the weak link in the security chain if you don't consider them, and by considering humans as the solution instead of the problem, you change the security outlook of your whole organization.

You'll see many of these concepts touched upon again through the book as we discuss cyber hygiene in a changing digital landscape.

Now, I want to take the time to review some of the risky behaviors that employees are prone to engaging in, and how it can compromise everything. In the next chapter, we'll discuss the most common pitfalls that employees tend to fall into, and how those seemingly trivial events can wreak havoc on your organization and your reputation—and, ultimately, your bottom line.

2

How Risky Behavior Leads to Data Breaches

Many employees have a lot on their plate and work hard to keep up with their rigorous job responsibilities. To meet the demands of their position, they create shortcuts to expeditiously accomplish their tasks and not get mired in the details. Herein lies the problem of risky employee behavior – in many cases, employees are not aware that their shortcuts or truncations of protocol are creating gaping holes in an organization's cyber hygiene. They may not mean to harm the organization, and their behavior is certainly non-malicious, but their risky behaviors have turned them into insider threats all the same.

This chapter is about this behavior and how it can lead to devastating outcomes. In reality, a great deal of this risky behavior can be stopped by creating cognizance around the implications of these actions. In most cases, employees are woefully unaware of the consequences of their actions, and what they don't realize is that a small error can quickly snowball out of control.

Even when employees know these behaviors are technically risky, they underestimate the risk of their actions and overvalue convenience.

In this chapter, we'll discuss some risky behaviors common to oblivious and negligent non-malicious insiders, and then we'll move on to how social media is often misused by employees of an organization. For each risky behavior, I'll make sure you know how to combat it effectively, and improve your organization's cyber hygiene.

Oblivious behaviors

We'll start by discussing the kind of behavior you might find from an oblivious, non-malicious insider threat. Oblivious employees aren't motivated by any desire to cause harm, or even by laziness or resistance to protocol; they simply don't understand that the actions they're taking, or forgetting to take, cause holes in their organization's security.

Unattended computers are a hazard

One classic form of oblivious behavior is leaving computers unattended when outside the organization – I've seen this many times at conferences, even security conferences. People go and check in their laptops along with their coats! They hand the laptop over for a checkout ticket, getting a false sense of security and trust because they've got the checkout ticket in their possession. That makes them feel like the laptop's safe; when really, it's been taken by an individual you don't know, to a place you can't see.

This happens at restaurants as well, and it's obviously risky behavior, especially for an executive. They might think that they don't want to bring the laptop case to their table because it's more secure with the checkout kid in the coat check. This is not a rational decision, but people can convince themselves of almost anything. In fact, I've seen people ask the bartender to put their devices under the bar. There's zero protection, but we've been socially engineered to think if it's OK for my coat, why not my computer? Let me make it clear—even in secure establishments, it's terrible cyber hygiene to leave your computer in somebody else's hands.

Many employees are under the impression that leaving a computer with someone else is totally fine as long it's off. This is a common mindset–if it's turned off, it's safe. In reality, that's patently false, as any computer can be accessed and hacked even when turned off, through a cold boot attack. Any device that has privileged company information on it needs to be locked down at all times when it's not in the hands of the designated employee.

Maintaining privacy while working remotely

Another risky behavior is not thinking about someone peering over your shoulder. Often, employees do not understand the need for privacy screens on computers, tablets, and smartphones when working remotely. This phenomenon becomes most problematic when working remotely on confidential documents in public places such as airports and coffee shops.

Employees need to understand that there are many ways for a breach to happen after some looks over your shoulder to see what you are working on. It only takes a few seconds for someone to grab your credentials, such as your username or password.

Even worse, they can use any information they can gather for a phishing or social engineering attempt. Avoid these pitfalls by investing in a privacy screen. It's an inexpensive and practical way to keep your documents and credentials confidential in a public setting.

Carrying around sensitive information

Yet another risky behavior that we see among employees is carrying around unnecessary sensitive or confidential data on one's computer, tablet, or smartphone. It's easy to imagine an employee who's finished a project, no longer views information about it to be sensitive because it's finished, and who doesn't bother to delete it from their device. Alternatively, think about what happens when an employee upgrades their device to a new one – and doesn't wipe the old one. This happens every day across the globe, as people sell used equipment that still contains sensitive information.

For example, there have been cases reported in which unwiped remote access equipment was sold online, and gave access to sensitive information that put the company at risk. That was only discovered due to the honest nature of the buyer. A worse scenario is what would happen if you sold a used VPN remote access kit that wasn't properly wiped. This could potentially give the buyer access to the entire network, with live data.

To reduce risk, protocol should be stringent, and demand full deletion of sensitive or confidential information the moment the employee does not need access to it. Human behavior is tied to meaningful information. If the information is no longer meaningful to an employee, the level of discretion and importance of protecting that information drops. Without a firm protocol to follow, it's easy to forget to delete "old" data, and eventually that will open up a straight line of access to someone who wants to lift that information.

Whether information is old or new, it remains very valuable in the eyes of a hacker. It's obvious why new information is valuable; but bad actors can also use old information to gain the trust of someone else within the organization. Leveraging that trust, they can gain access to everything, using intel acquired from seemingly outdated information.

The good Samaritan – beware of unintentional risky behavior

Another pitfall is an oblivious employee unintentionally becoming an attack vector themselves. For example, picture an employee driving to work on a Monday morning. They park their car and proceed to walk into the building. By the front door, they see a USB drive with the company logo printed on it. They pick it up thinking it may have some valuable company information on it. So, like a good employee, they walk it into the building and bring it to their office. Then they plug it into their computer to see what information was on there, in order to figure out which person needs their drive back. While the oblivious employee's intentions were honorable at every step, this remains a clear example of a non-malicious insider threat.

The USB in question could very easily be a hacker's way of social engineering their way into an organization. This is a simple but powerful social engineering technique, similar to the baby shower cake example. Something as simple as a USB drive with a company logo that became immediately trusted because of a logo. It **belonged**, it was **familiar**, it felt **safe**—never mind that the hacker loaded a USB with malware hoping an employee of the company would plug it into the network.

Betting on the "good Samaritan theory" – that a noble person would plug it into the network to identify its rightful owner, since it had the markings of the organization imprinted on it – it would seem, "the right thing to do." Best practice here would be to take the USB drive and deliver it to the security team in the organization and explain how and where it was found.

Negligent behaviors

Oblivious behavior is in some ways easier to deal with – the employee doesn't know that their behavior is threatening to the organization, and if they're educated properly and become part of a security culture, those behaviors will stop. Negligent non-malicious behavior, on the other hand, is when the employee knows that their action causes a security risk. They simply underestimate the risk, and overestimate the convenience of the risky action. These employees need to be convinced not just of what to do, but also of how important it is that they do it, and the possible consequences of not following the protocol.

Leaving the door open – the problem with recycled passwords

Coming up with a new password is often a task one faces without preparing for it – a reminder pops up and, suddenly, you need to invent a password. This leads to negligent employees using the same passwords and usernames that they've already used for websites and other accounts. This, unfortunately, is a very common problem in most organizations. More often than not, employees utilize the same two or three passwords and usernames across all their accounts, as well as the websites they visit.

These habits often jump from personal devices to company devices. People mistakenly believe that they can use the same username and password for both their personal and work life because they're not connected. After all, it can be hard to remember so many passwords and logins, so it's easier just to standardize them across the board.

Herein lies the problem: Bad actors can first hack unprotected or lightly protected websites to gain access to the list of usernames and passwords. After swiping that information, they can use this list for the real targets where they're hoping to gain access. Traversing these steps, they're counting on the fact that one or more accounts and their access will line up exactly.

Unfortunately, the prevalence of recycled passwords means hackers have pulled this off many times. For example, hackers used an employee's recycled password they obtained from a past LinkedIn breach to access information on 60 million accounts from Dropbox.

I've found it's incredibly important educate your employees about the dangers of reusing passwords and usernames. Instead, have them utilize a password-encrypted app or password minder if they have trouble remembering too many of them. You can also make use of multifactor authentication, which is an important, reliable vector for identity and trust.

Not to be shared – a password should remain secret

Another big problem you'll face is maintaining the personalization of your employees' passwords. A password is what is means – your access to where you need to go. Sharing passwords, especially administrative credentials, is a sure way to cause a breach. Even if you keep your passwords in an encrypted password keeper, you can't share them. When a negligent employee shares their passwords, they've just left another door open for the leakage of information through human error. Even with a trusted person, the chance of human error doubles when a password is passed to just one person other than the intended user.

Walking through executive suites on my way to deliver presentations, I've seen passwords on Post-it notes attached to the desks or screens of employees. Trying to lighten the mood while giving a stern warning, I would bring up how openly displaying passwords is a prime example of poor cyber hygiene. The misguided response was enough to make me cringe: putting passwords on Post-its was totally permissible, because it's the executive suite and only executives are allowed in this area. Therefore, they trusted employees who would traverse that allegedly secure area.

I could hardly believe their retorts. I pointed out that I was walking there freely, just like anyone else invited to meetings there. Scores of people likely did the same, and they would now have these passwords that could grant access to everything. Never mind the nightly cleaning crew, or any other third-party vendor who came to perform repairs or install something new. Access was right there for them as well, if they choose to use the information right in front of them.

This nearly comical blunder is seen in many kinds of organizations, including finance, healthcare, security, and many more. Entry into an organization's network can come from any point, even one as simple as a password on a lifted Post-it that was attached to a computer or desk.

The takeaway is clear: Never share passwords, and never keep them in a place where they can be lifted and used by others.

Failure to report a lost or stolen device

Another form of risky behavior arises when employees fail to report lost or stolen laptops, smartphones, or USB drives that contain confidential data in a timely manner. Employees might be dissuaded from reporting such an event because they're fearful of repercussions, afraid of losing their job, or didn't even realize that anything was missing. All three of these cases are negligent, but the first two are far more common.

I can't stress enough how much timely reporting is critical in minimizing the risk of a breach. The sooner the organization knows, the sooner they can act to protect themselves. Linking back to the discussion about training and global awareness steps to achieving cyber hygiene, it's imperative to have open and honest communication with all of your employees.

Having the foundational discussions around all areas including human error will prove to be very valuable. Lay the groundwork for an organization where employees understand that human error absolutely will occur, and when it does, they'll work together as a team to minimize the fallout and mitigate risk.

Unsecured Wi-Fi is a no-go

It might be convenient, but accessing Wi-Fi via unsecured wireless networks is a big no. This a common and commonly accepted protocol for employees to follow, but most people do it anyway, without taking a moment to realize the consequences of their actions.

In reality, it's a very risky behavior; but the draw to engage in this behavior, the sheer convenience, remains a powerful motivator. Imagine yourself sitting in a coffee shop, or at the airport and remembering those last few emails you just have to get out. Let's face it: VPN-ing is not at the forefront of your mind when you want instant access to Wi-Fi.

In fact, tests conducted around public Wi-Fi and the public's love for it have found that finding free Wi-Fi feels like a win in most people's book. There have even been instances where the Wi-Fi names were obviously malicious, like IwillStealYourData, IamAHacker, or DataGrabber, and even that didn't stop most people. People clicked on it to grab the free Wi-Fi without stopping to think if it was a smart choice to do so. For the bulk of folks, convenience and speed outweigh any thoughts around security.

No one has the mindset that they will be the ones to get hacked or breached. We often fall into the trap of wishful thinking that there have to be more compelling targets than us, and we can't be that important in the grand scheme of things. This line of thinking is incorrect.

In general, hackers cast a wide web and try to garnish as much information from as many people they can at once and will later attempt to make that data work for them. In sum, everyone who accessed these Wi-Fis are at risk.

To avoid creating unnecessary risk, always have your employees securely VPN in, and discourage public Wi-Fi use. In the end, grabbing information via a public Wi-Fi is just a popular and easy way into your organization for hackers to use. Another way into your organization, which makes use of a combination of oblivious and negligent behaviors by your employees, is social media.

Social media

Many people don't realize that social media is one of the biggest portals for data breaches, phishing attempts, and social engineering. Given that social media has many risks from many different vantage points and plays an outsized role in modern life, let's explore every angle of the risks in detail.

As a rule of thumb, when it comes to using social media within an organization, employees will feel secure for the most part because they believe that they're safe at work. From an employer perspective, organizations may be under the impression that by having a firewall they can stop access to some social media sites during work hours. Those who believe this have obviously not thought about the realities of living in an age of **BYOD** (**Bring Your Own Device**).

We all know BYOD has become very popular in recent years because we all do it. Many of us carry around two phones: a work phone and a personal phone. Inevitably, we bring both into the work environment. Perhaps we even bring our own laptop to the workplace, because we feel more comfortable on a device we purchased ourselves. BYOD means that any attempts to stop employee use of social media during work hours are probably dismal failures.

Social media use is inevitable, but the kind of oversharing that undermines your cybersecurity is avoidable. Your employees need to fully understand the risks involved in oversharing and how their innocent actions can have dire consequences.

When information is overshared, or privileged information is shared online, via social media, it typically falls under the non-malicious insider threat category. Management can attempt to monitor work accounts or handles, but in most cases they are unable to keep tabs on their employee's personal accounts. Much to the chagrin of cybersecurity professions, the vast majority of information leakage through social media comes from personal accounts when employees are on lunch break, weekends, or even on vacation.

Preventing oversharing

To prepare companies for this brave new world, I cofounded *SecureMySocial* several years ago. SecureMySocial is a technology-assisted self-monitoring tool for employers to give to employees, to help them self-monitor themselves across social media.

There is no big-brothering involved, with real-time warnings and auto-delete capabilities if authorized. You can group employee rules and notifications based on their section of the business, whether it's M&A, HR, Finance, and so on. Using that categorical information, rulesets are deployed that are applicable to them. Moreover, there are no false positives, and warnings are sent to the user's own choice of personal email or SMS.

The program reminds them, in real-time, if information was put out there that would cause data leaks or reputational harm to the organization. It then gives the employee the ability to rectify the situation all in real time, as rapidly reversing any type of leak as swiftly as possible is critical to minimize the risk and damage.

Remember that leakage of information is not typically malicious; it is a way of communicating and sharing. We live in a world where sharing is part of being present and belonging. The more we share, the more relevant we are, the more social we are, the more impact we have, the more we will be noticed and recognized, and the more we become part of the social community. Social media self-monitoring tools allow your employees to think for just a moment longer about what they're posting, and why; it doesn't take away their ability to use social media effectively. Constant sharing is a new area of social life, at the heart of Millennial and Gen Z culture, and it's not going away any time soon.

A real-life example of oversharing on Facebook

Some time ago, I came across an example of how someone can think they're engaging in harmless social media usage, when in reality they're oversharing, and creating an entry point for a breach. At the time, I was doing some consulting for a bank, which was implementing a new piece of internal security in its organization.

One of the bank's engineers, who was part of the implementation group, ran into some difficulty implementing the new security solution and getting it to flow through the organization.

How did he troubleshoot when he ran out of ideas? He did what he typically did when he had questions to be answered, or problems to be solved. He went onto Facebook, where he connected and communicated with a lot of his engineering friends. He posted his questions about the security issues and technological problems he was having while implementing the new security solution, and about the difficulty his team was having getting it to work. He asked if anyone worked with that particular security, and if they had, could they give him some pointers. To him it was an innocent act, merely asking his peers for advice, just so happening to use social media as his medium of communication. At this point, it's important that we don't just blame this guy for oversharing; the bank was not practicing proper cyber hygiene, and did not have appropriate security and communication protocols in place.

Take a moment and imagine the sheer size of the audience for this information, about exactly what new security was being put in place, and exactly what troubles the implementing team were having with it. In a moment, that information was made available to his friends, the friends of his friends, their family members, and so on. The number of people who now had access to all this information could be in the millions. It could have led to a devastating breach. To be clear, this security was never forward facing, and should never have been known by outside parties.

In this specific case, disastrous outcomes were avoided when the company was made aware of this serious breach of sensitive information. The company quickly decided to change the security being implemented, because of the nature of the information that was shared.

As you can see, oversharing can cause massive costs and inconvenience even if it's caught in time. In this case, disaster was averted at the last minute, but it certainly convinced the c-suite of the importance of cyber hygiene, and the tools and protocols their employees needed to use social media in a safer way.

Career-focused websites are conduits too

Another innocent example of oversharing on social media would be to give too much away on LinkedIn. You probably already know that LinkedIn is used as social media for professional networking, people looking for jobs, and organizations posting ads. In most cases, users of LinkedIn display their current job, their job history, schooling, awards, certifications, and current job description as well as a wealth of other information.

Most people like to be as descriptive as possible, sharing as much information about themselves as possible, for a number of reasons: networking, being relevant for headhunters approaching them for their next opportunity, socializing with the right groups, and so on.

In some cases, putting too much information about your current role in your LinkedIn profile can cause more harm than benefit. That's because identifying your exact role in a company can, in some cases, target you as a prime candidate for a phishing or hacking attack.

Bad actors scour social media, looking for the right tidbits of information to create profiles of the people that they think would most likely fall prey to an attack. They might gather information from similar accounts, and invite the target to be part of an exclusive networking group of like-minded individuals. Human nature means people want to belong, and even more so if it involves an exclusive invite-only club.

Another example would be for a bad actor to social engineer their way into the good graces of an employee. They can accomplish this by doing their homework on the company they are targeting, which is easily done on LinkedIn. Step one is to search the employees within the organization, get their names, information, job description, and title. From that information alone, our bad actor can then identify a few employees to social engineer.

Typically, the easiest route is for the bad actor to create a fake LinkedIn account, and make themselves an imaginary employee of the company they wish to infiltrate. Their job description and title would be a few levels up from that of the target.

They would then send the target a direct message saying something along the lines of "I've noticed your work on XYZ project (having grabbed that information from a little digging) and I would love to help you grow within the company," and then send then a LinkedIn request.

The targeted employee would likely approve the connection request, since they would be under the impression that the bad actor works for the same company, knows about project XYZ, and might be a person that they need to facilitate a move up the ranks of the organization. That paves the path to a breach that will greatly damage the organization.

One simple message on social media can lead to an avalanche

It all begins with one simple message that taps into the human factors of trust or want from the targeted employee. Once trust has been established, the bad actor can start requesting a bit more information each time they communicate, all with promises to help the employee move forward in their organization. These kinds of social engineering attacks and phishing attacks are very common; it's a simple use of social engineering, to find the weakest link in the security chain – the human – and use that weakness to break into an organization.

You can prevent a great deal of heartache by educating your employees about what's at stake. Have discussions with your employees about the dangers of phishing and social engineering, and teach them how to stay vigilant on social media. It is important to be clear in employee contracts about what they're allowed to list as their position within the organization, when they put it out there for public consumption on LinkedIn, Facebook, or any other social media.

For example, it's ok to say Director, Managing Director, or even VP, but getting too detailed may prove to be problematic. It's important to note that employees take their social media very personally even as it pertains to LinkedIn, so the best thing would be to make it part of an employee agreement when signing contracts, instead of trying to have a discussion with employees who have been working there for years.

Takeaway – practicing cyber mindfulness

As you'll have gleaned through these examples, when your employees engage in risky behavior, they can actively undermine the thorough security protocols that you've worked diligently to put in place. Employees must understand that when they leave their workplaces, their responsibilities to protect their organizations, as well as themselves, do not cease. Everyone within the organization must practice cyber mindfulness as a way of life, no matter where they are at any given moment. Just as traditional mindfulness encourages you to be aware of your surroundings and the consequences of your actions, cyber mindfulness involves being aware of your online connections and the consequences of your digital actions.

Even at a personal level, cyber mindfulness helps you protect every single facet of your life, including your career, reputation, and family. We live in a fast-paced world where we're constantly on the go, have many duties and desires pulling at us, and are completely connected to the technology around us. When we multitask, we are spread thin, which means we need to introduce the idea of pausing and thinking before we pull a digital trigger. When we act quickly to complete mundane tasks, we often do it without a lot of forethought. If "stop, pause, and think" were ingrained in our mindset, most of these risky behaviors would be curbed, or eliminated entirely.

Looking forward – breaking down cybersecurity through interviews

Over the next few chapters, we'll delve deeper by talking to the experts who will outline what you need to know about their respective fields within cybersecurity. After each interview, I'll discuss and distil these concepts to highlight critical takeaways that I personally believe will be game changers for your organization, and your cyber hygiene.

Cybersecurity is not a standalone concept, and these interviews and commentary reflect that reality. I approach the topic using as many real-world examples from my own career journey and from my interviewees' experiences as possible. These real-world anecdotes highlight problems with relatable and teachable moments, providing you with solutions that can help inform your decisions on how to approach these situations.

First, we'll tackle blockchain, a technology that's already changing the landscape of the digital world. But like any human creation, it's not foolproof. It's still in its infancy, and its real long-term impact remains to be seen.

3

Blockchain – The Unwritten Chapter on Cybersecurity

Blockchain is one of the most secure technologies ever invented, but one thing stands out when we look at its future – no one is sure of the exact ways immutable digital ledgers, securely distributed across multiple computers, could affect cybersecurity. In today's world, even at the c-suite level many people don't understand what blockchain is, what its potential impact could be, and what the future landscape of cybersecurity will look like as blockchain becomes embedded in our day-to-day processes. This chapter is forward-looking, and attempts to paint a picture of a world in the not-so-distant future, and how your organization can evolve to keep up with these rapid changes while transitioning to a sustainable 21st century business model that leverages this giant leap in technology.

Our two experts weigh in and talk about the present and future of blockchain with a heavy emphasis on how blockchain is already changing the rules of what it means to have effective cyber hygiene. Additionally, these interviews give us an insight into how the latest advancements of technology often work together. We can't think about blockchain without considering how it might overlap with AI, automation, and IoT.

Let's make something clear: we can't pretend to know where these technologies are going to take us and what their exact impact on cyber security will be. Much as the Internet changed the rules of modern life, these technologies will alter the way we work and live, in ways that we don't yet know. The cyber dimensions are yet unwritten, but many expect blockchain will make cybersecurity easier and more effective.

Blockchain isn't changing absolutely everything at once, even though it's naturally incredibly secure. Typical vulnerabilities can still undermine your security. Social engineering approaches, hardware exploits, and other existing security vulnerabilities mean that while blockchain has incredible security potential, it can't solve all our security problems due to the insecure world that surrounds it.

Guenther Dobrauz-Saldapenna

Guenther is a partner with PwC in Zurich and specializes in structuring, authorization, and ongoing lifecycle management of financial intermediaries and their products. A practicing tech and innovation enthusiast since 2002 he also strongly focuses on LegalTech, RegTech, and the fascinating blockchain space.

Shira Rubinoff: Could you talk a little about your background?

Guenther Dobrauz: I'm a partner at PricewaterhouseCoopers (PwC) in Zurich, Switzerland where I head up PwC Legal. I also serve on the global legal leadership team, where I have particular responsibility for all our LegalTech efforts globally.

After practicing with a leading law firm and in court, I started my career for real as a venture capitalist as part of the team at probably one of the first Swiss venture investment entities. After that, I moved to a managed futures fund, which was very much built around technology and risk management.

Today, my primary practice is around financial services and regulation thereof, but I also work extensively with the emerging blockchain technology here in Switzerland.

There are many start-ups, but institutions are also getting into this area. They work with us and I chiefly advise on the legal and regulatory aspects. I work very closely with our technology expert in the firm.

Cyber is increasingly entering into people's consciousness. We currently mostly deal with pure cybercrime, but we also think a lot about how technologies like blockchain might change the landscape and potentially even counteract what we're experiencing right now.

Shira Rubinoff: To set the stage, do you believe that innovative uses around blockchain are more prevalent in Europe than in the U.S.?

Guenther Dobrauz: I couldn't claim to have the full picture. What I can say is that in the old days, as a venture capitalist, I tended to look toward the U.S., especially California and other hotspots, where all the fascinating new technology was coming from.

So almost like a reflex that was also the first thing that I did when I saw blockchain emerging. But when it came to blockchain I found more innovation and growth in places like Estonia and Switzerland, which otherwise wouldn't necessarily spring to mind as the first places to look, which was quite surprising.

Why is that? I don't claim to have the full answer but part of the reason might be that when I talk to many companies, in particular in Silicon Valley, I quickly realize that they are built around centralization. The very idea of decentralization, which is important for blockchain, or variants thereof, doesn't resonate well with them. Perhaps this is why other countries with a long tradition and culture built around subsidiarity, decentralization, and consensus are becoming more important in this sphere.

Cyber awareness and identity measures are arising wherever the hotspots are and wherever a critical mass of talent is. It could just be that a more diverse global landscape is emerging and overtaking the established ones in the U.S. and UK.

As a final note on this, I couldn't put into words how impressed I was with some of the things I saw in Asia. We still tend to overlook that region and I believe that's a mistake.

Shira Rubinoff: Do you think that applications of blockchain technology will complement and advance cybersecurity or hinder it?

Guenther Dobrauz: I think the jury's still out on that. First of all, blockchain is a transformative technology like the Internet or electricity. It will become an infrastructure technology, but it will be transformative and not just disruptive.

Sometimes we don't even think about the transformative power of the Internet. To give an example, I can fly to Boston without ever having been to a travel agency. I can hail a taxi using the Internet and go to a hotel that I've rented from somebody I've never seen and never will see.

I believe that blockchain is going to have a similar trajectory and development to the Internet. I couldn't pretend to have the slightest idea of where blockchain is going to go and what the cyber dimensions will be.

Since we have experience from the Internet, we have an idea of the cyber risks that might rise in parallel with blockchain and what we need to do to counteract them. We didn't have this advantage with the Internet because we were still learning about the risks. I'm still surprised every day by how people use the Internet and how they are not conscious of the risks. This lack of awareness opens the floodgates for the cyber risks that we experience, unfortunately.

I hope that blockchain and cybersecurity will complement each other and that people will address them in parallel. I hope that cybersecurity will be easier with the blockchain-based solutions available to us.

Shira Rubinoff: Are there any stories that you can share about projects that you've worked on that combined blockchain technology with cybersecurity?

Guenther Dobrauz: It's a tricky one because first of all, this is all very new. We're talking about a timeframe of two years, or 30 months, in which we're seeing these sorts of things happening.

I've been involved with identity projects, which usually started with solving a problem. You can do a lot with digital identities once you have them. In the banking context, this may help with identity theft, phishing, and social engineering around that because it does get more complex and difficult for criminals if you have blockchain-based identity solutions.

We have created models trying to find solutions around the refugee crisis. The first step was dealing with it a bit more efficiently. We also tried to profile all those people and create evidence. When you do that, you realize that there's an entire shadowy world that includes human trafficking in the background.

This is where the boundaries blur between different realms of crime: human trafficking, identity theft, and so on. The opportunities to make a difference are so plentiful. We can't let people who want to abuse this technology take the lead. We must get ahead of the criminals and use it to our advantage to make the world better. That sounds a little naive, but it's my honest hope.

Shira Rubinoff: You read articles where companies or individuals are saying that blockchain's going to solve everything. People are saying that we're going to solve data privacy issues, supply chain issues, the Internet of Things (IoT) issues, and so on. Why do you think that people go around saying this? Is the future of blockchain in these areas?

Guenther Dobrauz: There are two reasons for saying these things. Some people really believe them. There are people like us: the geeks who get behind a new technology with typically honest intentions and a real fascination about it. We're at this stage focused on making technology out of money rather than money out of technology.

However, this is where the hype builds up and because of this, it quite often seems like people are saying, "I don't know what the problem is, but blockchain will be the solution."

That feels similar to when I started in the venture capitalist scene at the end of the '90s. At that point, everybody was trying to do everything with a .com attached to it, which then led to the boom and bust of the Internet bubble, which is quite often used as a comparison.

The story I always tell is that I was researching for what would later become my PhD thesis starting in 1998 and I was really struggling to find literature. Then I met this guy who was an IT geek, and he told me about this thing called the Internet. He said, "You can find things out there."

He gave me a list of domains to look at which I still have in a frame on my wall. One of the domains was amazon.com. The IT geek sold it to me as something where you put terms into a field and it would then spit out books.

I had no idea what Amazon would eventually become and for several more years I thought that Amazon was an extended library research tool. Bottom line is that the concept for Amazon was already there at the time, but for it to unfold the entire infrastructure needed to rise in parallel. And that I am probably not the best person at the Nostradamus game.

To conclude, I believe that we have no idea yet what blockchain is going to do. We're in the age of exponential technologies and it's at the intersection of those technologies where the magic will happen.

If you couple blockchain with IoT, or with artificial intelligence (AI), it's going to get exciting. That's too much for my little lawyer's brain to contemplate, but I think it's going to create a whole new world.

Where the Internet changes the way we interact, blockchain is going to change the way we transact and then again how we interact with people by building trust right into the systems. I think it could solve a lot of problems.

Shira Rubinoff: We talk frequently about collaboration in the area of cybersecurity to make things more fluid. Do you think emerging blockchain technologies could benefit from that same community effort?

Guenther Dobrauz: I think the entire spirit of blockchain is collaborative. There's that open-source mentality when you look at how the promoters of blockchain started. People get together in the same way as in the old days, I imagine. I wasn't there, but I imagine that people in Silicon Valley and other places had to collaborate and be very DIY.

All kinds of organizations, and sometimes ones that previously found themselves in fierce competition, are now collaborating because this technology needs to work. There's so much opportunity in this space for everybody. There's a different culture that goes with it, as well. I hope it will continue as such and not be hijacked by others too early, so we can continue to share and collaborate.

Shira Rubinoff: What would you say are the use cases around blockchain where we see the most advancement and the most promise?

Guenther Dobrauz: The most advanced things we are seeing right now are clearly in the financial services space. Cryptocurrency is also a force because that's where this started.

If you talk about blockchain on the street, one typical reaction is "drug dealers and the dark web." But if you talk a bit more specifically to people, their initial reaction is usually "bitcoin," because that's what people think about when they think about blockchain.

If you look into the financial services space, we've blueprinted the financial architecture and sort of overlaid it with the crypto industry. When you look at that, you realize that within five years, something amazing has been built. We've got exchanges, wallets, mining, interfaces, and so on. It's all moving toward institutional grade infrastructure.

Logistics is another example. In the past few weeks, we've heard the news of the biggest competitors in logistics working together. I believe it was DHL, UPS, and FedEx coming together to think about how they can use blockchain to reduce and merge the burden of governance in the system. We'll get more efficient Internet safety from that.

Blockchain is being used by farmers for cattle feeding and in Switzerland, it's starting to be used in the watch industry and the butter industry among others.

We also see blockchain being used in sustainability. People are thinking about wildlife preservation. Blockchain is popping up everywhere, but it's very early days.

I'm giving a lecture at a University of Applied Sciences in Switzerland. I do this twice a year, but literally every time I have to completely redo my talk because everything is moving so fast in this space. The further we go, the more interesting blockchain will become because it will become tangible and people will start to understand it.

One great example of blockchain being used is the music industry. It's a broken industry but not because people are being stupid; they're doing a great job.

This is an old industry. In my country, there used to be three radio channels that played 17 hours of music seven days a week, with seven or eight songs played an hour. Whatever it was, it created a list that you could send and money was collected.

Since the digital explosion has happened, all of this music has been played all around the world. This has just crashed down on the entire industry. Some estimations say that, if ever even collected, it takes five to six years for money to reach those entitled to it: the artist, the producer, and so on. There's huge inefficiency in the industry and many people are leaving it.

If you add blockchain into the mix, that provides ownership. The industry can use a cryptograph from the moment the music is played. Money can be allocated to those entitled to it and you can take away all of the inefficiency in the middle, which will allow people to go back to doing what they love.

Shira Rubinoff: Do you believe that blockchain could provide complete security, eliminating the need for other cybersecurity measures, or does it need additional cybersecurity implementations to remain truly secure?

Guenther Dobrauz: Blockchain is man-made and it can be broken. This is one of the promises of blockchain that I don't subscribe to. People say that it's immutable and it can never be hacked; that's what we believe right now, but trust me, it can be broken. Somebody will find a solution.

We must put cybersecurity around blockchain because the one amazing and compelling thing about blockchain is that it has the potential to put trust into technology, systems, and infrastructure. If this trust is violated because there are cyber concerns, then the entire point of blockchain goes away.

The Internet is not the perfect comparison, but I remember a discussion that I had with my father a couple of years back when e-banking started. He said that he didn't trust it. A couple of years later, he was doing everything online, but he needed to trust it first.

Eventually, the hacking started, and we had the first instances where e-banking systems were hacked, and then people got shaken up. It took a while for us to regain trust. I absolutely believe that we must come up with solutions for cybersecurity so that we don't risk the potential of blockchain.

Shira Rubinoff: Do you have any last thoughts around blockchain?

Guenther Dobrauz: With all of my speeches, and even with my latest book, I include a quote at the beginning. It's from the Burning Man festival, and it goes, "The appropriate response to new technology is not to angrily retreat into the corner hissing and gnashing your teeth: it's to ask 'Okay, how should we use this?'"

I think this is the approach we've got to take. I don't believe that blockchain is going to solve all the problems out there in the world, but I also don't believe that it's going to be the devil and is going to destroy jobs.

It's a new technology and we just have to be open to it, look at it objectively, and get behind it to do amazing things.

I believe it's truly the privilege of a generation to live through the unfolding of a disruptive and/or transformative technology. We've experienced this with the unfolding of the Internet, and we're still experiencing it. I believe that blockchain has similar potential.

There's a big opportunity for decentralization with blockchain. Most of the problems that we have on this planet start with centralization. Typically, someone is being corrupt. There's always a single point of entry where something goes wrong. This is where blockchain can help because you have decentralization in there and the trust element. We must be as conscious of the risks as we are of the opportunities, but I believe that blockchain has the potential to help with our efforts to build a better world.

Shira Rubinoff: Thank you, Guenther Dobrauz.

Sally Eaves

Sally is the Social Impact lead for the UK Government Blockchain Association and contributes to parliamentary policy thought leadership. She was an inaugural recipient of the Frontier Technology and Social Impact award, presented at the United Nations in 2018, and is now leading major initiatives in this area, including presenting at Davos and leading events worldwide. She specializes in the application and integration of blockchain, AI, and associated emergent technologies for business and societal benefit.

Shira Rubinoff: Could you say a little about yourself?

Sally Eaves: I'm the CEO and Founder of an organization called Aspirational Futures that harnesses STEAM learning alongside emergent technologies, especially blockchain and AI, for social impact at scale. With my background as a chief technology officer (CTO), I also advise organizations globally on how to evaluate, apply and integrate advanced technologies, notably 5G, AI, and Secure Distributed Ledgers.

I enjoy working at the cutting edge with business alongside focusing on the wider societal perspective – indeed, I believe these can and must be combined. I am very passionate about how we can use technology for good. Much of my work history has seen this combination of advancing education and advancing emergent technologies. I regard this approach as the biggest driving force for digital transformation.

I also have a strong research background. I like to create opportunities to break down silos and bring together different perspectives across the different stakeholders. This is how I believe we can inform and scale meaningful change.

Shira Rubinoff: How long have you been in this sector?

Sally Eaves: Alongside my professorship in emergent technologies, I spent over 15 years in roles such as CTO, particularly working in telecommunications with organizations such as EE, Orange, and T-Mobile.

I have focused on the human side of technology and how we manage people and culture alongside any change, along with the hands-on implementation of technology and driving awareness.

Shira Rubinoff: You're at the forefront of people who are discussing and involved in blockchain technology. Do you see blockchain as a disincentive to cyberattacks?

Sally Eaves: One of the things I am asked about the most is where we're going with advanced technologies and their integration. Cybersecurity and blockchain are right up there as top discussion points.

For me, the key aspect of blockchain, and why it will make such a difference here, is decentralization. There is no single point of entry and that will be the biggest deterrent. Also, if there is a hack and entry is made, we will not have the issue, for example, of an entire repository of data being available from that one attack alone.

We are also looking at areas such as decentralized storage. Today data really is currency. We have a mass of sensitive data being shared, particularly in healthcare, and blockchain can be introduced as a major deterrent in this space.

I want to mention Internet of Things (IoT) security too. I always look for where the biggest weaknesses are in any system. Currently this is around our edge devices, for example switches, cameras, smart doorbells, and smart thermostats. We need more cybersecurity rigor at the edge – blockchain has a big role to play with IoT and can be harnessed to help protect these devices and their data exchanges from attacks.

Shira Rubinoff: How can blockchain support enterprises in addressing cyber risk challenges?

Sally Eaves: This is all about looking within the enterprise at where single points of vulnerability are as this is where blockchain can make a massive difference. The most recent examples are on the DNS side. If we want to store domain information immutably on a distributed ledger we can use blockchain, and the connection can be enabled by immutable smart contracts.

I have been advising several organizations recently that have been directly impacted by DNS attacks. In each case, the attack had caused havoc because there wasn't the response planning already in place to deal with it. The problem for these companies wasn't just the fact that cybersecurity and solutions such as blockchain had not been considered: it was also a communications issue.

Technology is one defense to incoming attacks but it is equally important to bring together the right stakeholders and have the right education embedded in advance. The point is that even if you have something ready that mitigates risk, you may not necessarily have the right communications in place to have the right people talking and the right action planning happening. Companies must practice what to do for when, and not if, these situations arise.

Shira Rubinoff: It's been said that implementing blockchain takes away the need for humans. What would you say to that?

Sally Eaves: Blockchain can negate or remove the need for human intermediaries in specific contexts, for example, related to auditing – but no, I do not believe that we are taking humans out of the equation. Like most emergent technologies and their integration, with ethical development we are talking more about a human-machine partnership.

There also remains a massive conflation between blockchain and cryptocurrency, which is an awareness barrier to the technology becoming mainstream. People can often quite understandably assume blockchain, bitcoin, and various altcoins are the same thing when they are not. The problem is that practical and accessible use cases have been limited and typically focused around the financial services space or auditing, but blockchain is so much more than that. We need greater awareness so that people can see the application relevance in their everyday work and personal life.

I have several courses coming out shortly for different types of audiences and experience levels. Many of these are free to access because I passionately care about opening up access to this type of information.

When technology projects go astray in any industry, it is typically the human factors that tend to be the biggest points of failure. This is the same for blockchain – understanding is key for people to buy in and must be embedded in any transformational change initiative.

We also need to build trust levels dramatically. Research has shown that trust is at a global 17-year low. This is not just related to some of the major stories that we have all seen in the news, such as that with Cambridge Analytica and Facebook. There's a lack of trust across many different sectors including charity. Blockchain is a way of embedding trust back into the system for human benefit.

Shira Rubinoff: People are also worried that automation will replace humans. I actually think it will only help humans to process information better by taking away the menial tasks. What's your view on combating negative preconceptions?

Sally Eaves: It's a question of changing the narrative and getting more balanced information out there and broadly accessible so that people can make informed choices. With blockchain, many of the early articles were sponsored by an exchange, which can be unhelpful because it conflates blockchain only with cryptocurrency, as I mentioned earlier.

People will always wonder whether information is biased, so the more quality information that's accessible to a range of audiences, the better. This information should not just be held in traditional technology magazines either.

If we look at the history of technology change, there have always been waves of technological advancement. Some jobs will disappear or be significantly changed as part of these changes, that is naturally part of the process. But certainly, new types of jobs and roles will be created too. One area we do need to pay close attention to is the ethical development of technology.

This includes ensuring diverse teams are building AI and taking the action needed to identify if any specific group may be more adversely affected by automation that another – then the steps can be taken in advance regards reskilling or upskilling for example.

Additionally, when we are looking at blockchain, AI, and the integration of frontier technologies, "extra time" will be created. As you said, it's about taking away some of the routine, predictable, and mundane tasks. What can we do with that extra time that is far more meaningful? I think this is very exciting.

I often work with the United Nations (UN) and focus on how technology can be harnessed for good. I thoroughly believe in what we can achieve with technology for social impact at scale. If I can leave a legacy in the world, it will be this.

I am working on projects that are using blockchain, for example, in supply chains. This leads to fair, ethical, and sustainable trade, along with ensuring food provenance. In many countries, people are losing out at every stage of the supply chain, from farm to fork. Through blockchain, AI, or other technology integration, we can find a way to solve this. I am especially passionate about two projects – one using blockchain to provide identity and access to financial services for the 1.7 billion people worldwide that are unbanked or under-banked. Another is using blockchain and other technologies to combat trafficking.

Shira Rubinoff: Earlier we discussed how blockchain can support enterprises in addressing leading cyber risk challenges. Are there areas that are inherent within blockchain's characteristics that really go against this?

Sally Eaves: I would never say blockchain is a panacea. We are moving at a rapid pace of progress, but we are not there yet. There are some challenges that need to be addressed. One of them is resource intensity, for example around mining costs and computer power. There are also issues around legacy systems and legacy coding, particularly in data center environments.

Another issue is reversibility in financial services. One of my former roles as a CTO was with a major telecommunications company.

When certain issues happened with a new release, we sometimes had to do rollbacks. With blockchain technology, to be able to do something like that you need a consensus over a number of nodes. That becomes inherently very difficult.

Shira Rubinoff: How would you describe the current maturity level of blockchain technology with particular reference to cybersecurity?

Sally Eaves: We're seeing much more movement out of the laboratory and with early pilots that are going live. We now have real-world data coming through that we can measure and evaluate. This means we are right at a tipping point. We're on the cusp of the actualization rather than just conceptualization side of change. That's a great place to be. I also feel that the quality of people and projects involved in this space is rising all the time.

Shira Rubinoff: Do you think there's any specific sector that's leading the charge forward in blockchain technology?

Sally Eaves: Yes, I would say two sectors – financial services and supply chain. We are going to see more development in both, but I would love to showcase a sector outside of this too: healthcare.

I am seeing a lot of research and development focused on the "marriage" of AI and blockchain technologies. As an example, we have an opportunity to use blockchain as a method of security for our DNA data, negating fears of it being misused – while AI can enable rich insights to be anonymously extracted from it. This combination is critical to give people confidence and control about sharing their data and potentially its monetization, which could be transformational in developing economies. Our health data is the most sensitive data we have. It's also of universal interest and importance as we all have people we love and want to look after. That makes it personal. Enabling an increase in data volume and data quality for research studies is of specific interest. We have a shortage of data for specific diseases and conditions, and some ethnic minority groups. I see blockchain as a democratizer of data for both business and societal good.

Shira Rubinoff: How do you feel AI should fit within an optimal cyber risk program?

Sally Eaves: Increasing numbers of companies are stating that they want to introduce AI and machine learning into their cybersecurity plans. But many companies or executives within are still saying that they do not actually know how AI works or what it does; they just know it's important. I mention education frequently because I believe this is critical – we have a disconnect between awareness and the specifics of technology and how it can be best applied.

Planning is critical, and learning is a big part of this process. There can be specific training around optimizing processes for managing cyber risks. There can also be broader training involving everybody in an organization. There needs to be this two-pronged approach to best enable effective cyber risk management.

Employees need to feel informed and empowered to recognize and deal with potential threats. I have done some work developing response plans: technology is a key part of this but it's also important that people feel prepared. This can be achieved by involving different stakeholders.

A key problem is that the level of innovation shown by attackers is rising all the time. The more we're going digital, the more our threat surfaces are increasing, especially at the edge. We need to have an open dialog about exactly what we want to mitigate, manage, and defend.

Shira Rubinoff: There's a lot of talk about who's responsible for the security in an organization. The chief operations officer (COO) is often moving things along quickly, whereas the chief information officer (CIO) wants to slow down, test, and implement proper security. With digital transformation, there needs to be a balance. Does blockchain fit into that? Is there a way that it can help people with different priorities to work together?

Sally Eaves: Yes, trust, open dialogue and bringing together a diversity of perspectives is critical to this balance. We also need to consider technology shelf-lives and the rate of change. I do not think we always appreciate the potential for some of our communications from today, to be intercepted and stored ready for developments "tomorrow." When advancements like quantum computing progress to actualization, some very sensitive communications data could be decrypted at that later time. This again returns to the importance of planning and foresight activity.

With quantum computing for example, there are many different theories about how many years it will be before it comes into active play. But in terms of risk, encryption, and the capacity to be hacked now and in the future, we need to pay attention in the here and now. This is not something that we can simply watch and wait for.

Shira Rubinoff: Are you saying that you can't just be reactive when it comes to security and cybersecurity?

Sally Eaves: Yes, particularly in terms of blockchain. Currently blockchain cryptography relies on something called prime number factorization and the linking of public and private keys. But with quantum computing, the private key information could be taken from the public key data.

At the moment, we lack the computing power to be able to do that without it taking quite literally years and years, but with quantum computing, transaction processing can be done so much quicker. Even with network effects, the implication of this is huge and the potential to hack comes to the fore. This must be considered right here and right now. If we want to do an upgrade to a blockchain-underpinned system to negate that risk, we need to ensure that consensus is reached because we cannot just flick a switch.

Technology is dualism and it's all about intent at the end of the day – it can be used for good or ill. The word people often use about quantum is "fear," but the advances that quantum can potentially bring, and the challenge that will provide for blockchain technology, is an amazing opportunity to enhance what we can do with cybersecurity and make it better still.

Shira Rubinoff: Is there any cutting-edge research in this space that you could share?

Sally Eaves: One thing I want to highlight is the Quantum Resistant Ledger (QRL). Although this is very niche and not many people are talking about it yet, I think it is highly significant. The QRL is a project and piece of research that's very applied in focus.

It assumes that quantum computing is here right now. I love this approach because it means we are not just watching and waiting. If we assume that quantum computing is coming in the next three months, how can we be ready for it? What do we need to understand? How can we develop a blockchain solution, for example, that is resistant to quantum or negates quantum's impact? It's about trying to complete a rapid development curve in a very agile way. I love to highlight developments like these that are perhaps "under the radar" but very valuable to know, discuss, and share.

Another one to look out for is happening in a region in Italy called Lombardy. They have invited outside voices to contribute to research about the future of emergent technologies and how this can be a catalyst for innovation, research, and technology transfer. These researchers are not just trying to make this a technology conversation; they're having a mainstream conversation about how technology matters to people. It is a great example of inclusive collaboration.

Similarly, I've been working with the University of Edinburgh to look at the next stage of technology – "The Six Ages." This includes everything we've been talking about today: research into blockchain, AI, IoT, quantum, and beyond.

Shira Rubinoff: Are there any of your personal blockchain projects that you're particularly excited about right now?

Sally Eaves: I am working on something that is going to massively push the boundaries of what we can do with blockchain. This project, associated with my Aspirational Futures initiative, will deliver blockchain and AI education, access, and implementation to meet specific UN Sustainable Development Goals across 5,000 cities in just three years.

This project is at the heart of everything that I believe we can do with technology with a huge number of international and cross-sector stakeholders involved. There's legacy work here too, which is always complex, but I believe that we are really going to push the envelope for positive lasting change.

I want to showcase how we can integrate some of the leading frontier technologies of our time. These are important not just for digital transformation in businesses but for societal transformation too. In fact, these go hand in hand. This is all about integration on a truly sustainable and scalable level.

I aspire that this project will make people curious, informed, and inspired to become more involved, develop their skills and experience, and ultimately be far more optimistic about what technology can do – and apply this for good.

Shira Rubinoff: Thank you, Sally Eaves.

Discussion

Our experts guided us through the promises and pitfalls of blockchain before they arrived at conclusions about technological integration, along with forward-thinking predictions about advances such as quantum computing. Let's begin with their thoughts on blockchain and the benefits and drawbacks of this technology as it pertains to cybersecurity. Later, I'll review how blockchain might work in concert with other technological advances such as AI, IoT, and automation to change the way we approach the way we adhere to our cyber hygiene.

Getting buy-in to blockchain

By design, blockchain is decentralized and that is its biggest promise. Typically, a bad actor has a single entry point, and with blockchain it is more difficult to wreak as much havoc since decentralization eliminates the single entry point. That means that a single hack won't be able to steal an entire repository of data. Still, even with these inherent advantages, we're still not sure whether blockchain with help or hinder cybersecurity, because while blockchain remains secure, people are not.

Blockchain is a transformative technology, but the cyber risks associated with it will undoubtedly increase, as they do for every technology as it gets adapted and widely used. Even today, people engage in risky behavior with older technology; two decades after the dawn of the internet, Guenther points out that many people are still careless with their online behavior. This is where the human factors of cyber hygiene are relevant.

Blockchain possibly holds the power to revolutionize the world, but Guenther reminds us that it remains a human creation, and as such, can be broken by other humans. Nothing is unhackable, and eventually, someone will find a way to compromise anything that's allegedly uncompromisable.

Understanding the pitfalls is key for people to buy into blockchain technology. The human factors must be embedded as blockchain is implemented into your organization. This begins with a broad understanding of the technology, which serves as the basic building block of enabling the transformation.

Sally echoes a sentiment that's discussed throughout the book, that human factors tend to be the biggest points of failure in cyber security systems. This is equally true of blockchain.

It's critical to create guard rails as you implement blockchain, since there's a lot at stake for the technology. Blockchain's reputation is on the line. If the technology is publicly compromised and a scandal tarnishes its image, it will damage the perception of the technology and delay its adoption en masse.

Think about recent developments around trust and how that influences the way technologies are being rolled out. Sally explains that human trust in change, technology, and other humans is at a 17-year low, and points out some of the many scandals that have created this type of broad sentiment. Because there's a lack of trust across many different sectors, we have to be extra careful as we integrate blockchain into our daily reality.

High hopes – the future of blockchain

We should be aware of parallels between 90s-era thinking that determined anything with .com at the end was pure unfettered magic, and today's wild expectations about blockchain. But we should still be forward thinking by viewing blockchain as a solution to many of the trust issues we have in cyber security. Blockchain, according to Guenther, will change the way we transact and interact with other people, and we shouldn't underestimate the impact that will have on the way we operate our businesses.

I believe that blockchain will help reinvent the way we collaborate, and that in itself will deliver promising solutions for cyber security problems. Because this technology is in its infancy, you should be open to collaborating with your industry peers and exploring how to avoid mistakes that other organizations have already made.

For instance, at the intersection of blockchain and cybersecurity are the incipient projects that Guenther mentions are just rolling out. One of them focuses on digital identity issues especially as it relates to banking. Theoretically, with blockchain-based identity solutions, you could prevent a great deal of financial crime from ever occurring.

Still, we need to be realistic and realize that contrary to what some are saying, blockchain isn't a cure-all for our most pressing cybersecurity challenges. In many cases, we're hyping up blockchain because it's the latest and greatest, and it can solve nearly any problem – even if we're uncertain about the parameters of the problem. We should keep our expectations about blockchain within reason.

Sally stresses that one area that needs to be prioritized is the ethical development of technology. As new technology gets integrated into our workflow, there will be entire swaths of the population that will be adversely affected by automation, and many of their positions will be reduced if not eliminated entirely.

We need to think big picture when this happens at our organizations: If we just dismiss those whose jobs are obviated, think about what type of nightmare we will be creating on a global scale. Instead of just disposing of these legions of workers whose skills are now outdated, it's critical to retrain them, through reskilling or upskilling. We can tap our existing talent pools and modernize them for our new automated reality, and convert that extra time into investing into our cyber hygiene.

Possible practical uses of blockchain

In fact, we should be excited about the "extra time" that will be created, as Sally mentioned. If we reduce or eliminate mundane tasks through automation, think about how much more you could do as an organization in a given day. Your organizational capacity is going to skyrocket, and with that expanded bandwidth, the possibilities for profit growth and impact grow as well. That extra time can easily be invested into improving your cyber hygiene and ensuring your organization has a proactive and reactive security stance, and always prepared for any threat that can come its way.

We should also be enthused at what blockchain can do for charitable endeavors. In today's world, people want to do social good, but there is always the possibility of having bad actors hijack and take advantage of people's kindness, to reap benefits from tragedies. Blockchain is a way of embedding trust back into the system for human benefit.

For example, the combination of blockchain and cybersecurity could change the outcome of the ongoing global refugee crisis, where it's hard to keep track of people as they move within countries and across international boundaries. Blockchain could help governments, relief agencies, and other organizations stay ahead of the criminals who prey on these vulnerable populations.

Blockchain and other technologies

We've seen how blockchain is one technology that can have exciting prospects, especially when paired with other technologies like the Internet of Things (IoT) and artificial intelligence (AI). Here's the problem: many yet don't understand how these technologies work themselves, never mind how they overlap in a modern context.

In the future, blockchain could help bolster your cyber defenses, especially when it comes to technology integration. For example, IoT is amazing, but it creates major weaknesses in systems, especially with edge devices such as switches, cameras, smart phones, and thermostats. Blockchain could help protect these devices and close these loopholes to keep out bad actors.

The same idea applies to AI: we need to understand what it is and how it works. Sally highlights the importance of understanding AI, as many folks in the c-suite are still woefully unaware of what AI does or how it actually functions. Naturally, if key people at the highest echelons of your organizations are in the dark about AI, rank and file is probably going to be very unsure of the implications of AI for your business and the nature of AI in general.

An effective organization that practices proper cyber hygiene would be quite the opposite: All employees, no matter their title, would be empowered to understand their technologies and fully ready to tackle cyber risks as they present themselves. Bad actors are relentlessly hustling and innovating to break their way into your systems; in order to keep up with the proliferation of threats, you must have organization-wide planning and foresight.

The world is changing rapidly, and your security posture has to evolve with it and keep up with the changing landscape. We're moving into the era of quantum computing, and for many, it's hard to understand how that's going to affect the world of cyber security.

Quantum is a word that evokes fear in cybersecurity professionals, but like any other technology it's a double-edged sword. As technology progresses, both cyber hygiene and threats will evolve, and it's incumbent on us to keep up these promising technologies.

While we don't know exactly what the future will bring, we do know that we have to fight the innovation of bad actors with innovation of our own. Inherently, technological integration between the best available advances is key to keeping up with the changing nature of threats. Hackers will leverage the best available technology and continually play a cat-and-mouse game to breach your defenses. That will never change, but in the future both sides will employ ever more sophisticated technology against each other to achieve maximum effectiveness. If you don't keep up, you're going to get left behind and fall victim to bad actors who are ahead of your cyber defenses.

Summary

As you've gathered through these interviews and commentary, the exact impact of blockchain on cybersecurity remains unwritten and will continue to reveal itself over time. We're already seeing how blockchain holds a great deal of promise for a multitude of uses across a wide variety of industries. I believe blockchain will likely be an important component in the cybersecurity of tomorrow, and that's why this forward-looking chapter explored some of the possibilities of this technology.

Still, future-looking prognostications sometimes blind us to the realities that will likely still govern the possibilities of new technological progress. That's why it's important to consider the high likelihood that blockchain isn't going to fundamentally alter the realities that encapsulate our world. Human factors that facilitate poor cyber hygiene are going to remain a problem.

In the end, blockchain isn't the panacea for every single one of our cybersecurity weaknesses. Nevertheless, blockchain remains a powerful tool, the future uses of which we will continue to discover as our security challenges continue to evolve, and we fight to keep our data safe.

4

Cybersecurity in the Cloud – What You Need to Know

One of the major technology trends of recent years has been the migration to "cloud computing" – that is, rather than businesses owning and hosting all of the equipment and data centers needed to run their information systems, they effectively outsource the responsibility for the infrastructure to others. Businesses may utilize virtual machines on rented servers sitting at a third-party provider, or may use Software as a Service – paying to use third-party web-based applications rather than have to implement similar systems in house. They may sync and store files at a remote provider, or backup to a cloud-based provider using software that automatically runs and manages the backup processes. Of course, these four examples are just a few of the many exciting advances that cloud computing has created.

Additionally, cloud computing has clearly brought tremendous entrepreneurial benefits to the market – the cost of starting up a new technology business today is typically much smaller than it was a decade ago; companies can effectively rent what they use to have to buy, and can pay only a small fraction of the support costs of shared systems.

But with the arrival of such conveniences come serious security concerns – for example, that sensitive data is no longer under the complete control of its owners, and that cloud technology transforms its providers into digital gold mines for hackers. Understanding the interplay between the cloud and cybersecurity is therefore critical – it can allow us to leverage the benefits of cloud without assuming unacceptable levels of risk.

With those concerns in mind, I reached out to Kevin Jackson and Jim Reavis, both experts in this area, to find out what critical security concerns exist in cloud computing. Their insight and industry knowledge are indispensable as they are both trailblazers in the cloud computing space.

Kevin L. Jackson

Kevin L. Jackson is a globally recognized cloud computing expert, thought leader, industry influencer, and author of the award winning *Cloud Musings* blog. He has also been recognized as a "Top 100 Cloud Computing Influencer and Brand" (Onalytica 2017) and a "Top Federal IT Blog" (FedTech Magazine 2015, 2016).

Kevin has been certified as an instructor by the International Information Systems Security Certification Consortium (ISC2), National Cloud Technologist Association and the Cloud Credential Council.

He holds an MS in Computer Engineering from Naval Postgraduate School, an MA National Security and Strategic Studies from Naval War College, and a BS Aerospace Engineering from the United States Naval Academy.

Shira Rubinoff: What is the most critical aspect of cloud security?

Kevin L. Jackson: The most critical aspect of cloud security is really understanding the organization's data. Many organizations think that understanding the sensitivity of the data (that is, low, medium, or high sensitivity) is good enough. That couldn't be further from the truth.

Sensitivity of data is just one aspect of understanding and knowing your data. You need to understand things like: where can the data go? For instance, you have data sovereignty laws that restrict the flow of data across borders. You need to understand if the data is associated with legal contracts because there may be related restrictions on the data.

You must understand if the data is personally identifiable data, because personally identifiable data needs to be handled in different ways in different jurisdictions, and in different countries. You also need to understand what is personal or sensitive data. In some countries, the very fact of your religion can get you killed, so that could be very sensitive information and something that you may need to protect if that data is in a certain country.

One of the most important domains is: who owns the data, because the data may not be owned by the organization. You may need to get approval from the owner of the data, which in many cases may be an individual.

You need to understand the context around how the data was collected. Most recently, with the EU General Data Protection Regulation (GDPR), many websites started telling people about the data being collected based on cookies. That was about providing a context for the data. If you get data for one purpose, you cannot use it for another purpose. So, this is yet another reason or way to understand your data. This is true not just for data you are going to collect going forward, but for all of your legacy data as well. So, this could be a very costly and a very difficult task.

Another very critical aspect of knowing your data is "How long should you keep the data?" There are legal and regulatory requirements that dictate how long organizations can hold data. After that period has elapsed, remaining data just presents more risk to the organization. This additional risk could lead to more cost driven by protecting data that you don't really need. That's yet another area where you need to classify your data.

These are all aspects of classifying your data that you need to know about. In fact, best practice is to classify your data across a minimum of 10 different domains.

Shira Rubinoff: How would you advise organizations to classify their data in a cost-effective manner, and what steps should they take to get there?

Kevin L. Jackson: The Cloud Security Alliance is an industry organization that has actually focused on the most cost-effective way of protecting data. It has developed a table called the Cloud Controls Matrix (CCM), which provides a list of 133 security controls over 16 separate domains that describe the most important data security controls. These controls are also cross-referenced with some of the major security governance documents globally, like the Federal Risk Authorization and Management Program (FedRAMP), ISO/IEC 27001, Health Insurance Portability and Accountability Act of 1996 (HIPAA), and others.

CCM is a tool that can use an organization's business model, business process, and industry, to identify the industry recommended security controls needed to protect each data type. By using this tool, companies can reduce risk and enable a focused data protection regimen. The enterprise can then add organization-specific requirements. By properly classifying data and matching the classification to these controls, your company can have a cost-effective process of protecting not only your current data and the data that you are creating, but your legacy data as well.

Shira Rubinoff: What controls do you need to have in place, from a cybersecurity perspective, to classify your data?

Kevin L. Jackson: The specific controls are provided by the Cloud Controls Matrix, but the key philosophy around these controls is that they cannot be static.

The traditional security model has been a very static model based on the protection of the infrastructure. In that model, the threat was barred from entering protected areas. Once you were validated or verified as being part of the organization, then you essentially had access to all of the information. That was also useful when your data was in a single location and this location was something that you managed as the organization's own data center.

Now the entire concept of work has changed from being a single location to being everywhere: mobility, mobile devices, the ability to work at home, and so on. This means that workers don't go to the data; the data has to go to the workers. So, in order to protect that data, security controls need to travel with the data. This means a shift from an infrastructure-centric security model to a data-centric security model.

The controls themselves need to interpret the context of how the data is being used as well as the location of use. You not only have to understand the business process using the data, but also user or the role and device that's accessing that data. You have to know the physical location of that data because that drives the legal and regulatory requirements for the protection of that data. Only by knowing your business process, the actual role, device and the location of that data can you select, implement, and enforce the required controls.

Shira Rubinoff: How do you enable and enforce the security controls in the cloud when you don't own the cloud itself?

Kevin L. Jackson: This is a very important question because it's based upon doing appropriate due diligence of your cloud service provider. One of the broadly recognized failures of organizations is when they don't do effective due diligence in assessing and choosing a cloud service provider (CSP). The enterprise needs to understand what security controls can be provided by the CSP; the answers could be based on geography or legal jurisdiction. Corporate leaders must also understand what metrics are associated with the ability of that provider to implement those controls. You also must be able to monitor those controls, and you need to understand and appreciate the concept of shared responsibility when it comes to security because it's not all on the CSP's shoulders. There are some controls that have to be implemented by the user or the consumer. Those controls need to be specified within the organization's governance and the CSP service level agreement (SLA). This is one of the major failures of organizations: not implementing appropriate data security governance based on the use of cloud services.

Shira Rubinoff: How do you implement, monitor, and enforce cybersecurity in this ever-changing dynamic environment?

Kevin L. Jackson: When you design, build, and deploy IT, you need to do it in a manner that recognizes not only continuous change but a heterogeneous environment.

Everything doesn't go into the cloud and all your data won't be in the cloud. Your organization may have managed service providers, legacy data centers, and entire business ecosystems with other partners. Executives will need to evaluate every one of those environments. All of this needs to be based on a consistent governance model, and the implementation and appropriate rewards to your organization for following and implementing that governance.

Companies must be able to monitor the implementation and effectiveness of security controls in a continuous manner. This is normally referred to as "continuous monitoring" and this involves identifying specific security metrics that all business ecosystem members use and report. With a cloud service provider, this is done based on service-level agreements; understanding the cloud service agreement; and putting specific requirements in your contract based on your own IT data and data classification activities.

Shira Rubinoff: Thank you, Kevin L. Jackson.

Jim Reavis

For many years, Jim Reavis has worked in the information security industry as an entrepreneur, writer, speaker, technologist, and business strategist. Jim's innovative thinking about emerging security trends have been published and presented widely throughout the industry and have influenced many.

Jim has been an advisor on the launch of many industry ventures that have achieved a successful M&A exit or IPO. Jim is widely quoted in the press and has worked with hundreds of corporations on their information security strategy and technology roadmap. Jim has a background in networking technologies, marketing, product management, and systems integration.

Shira Rubinoff: What is your work history and what projects are you working on right now?

Jim Reavis: I'm a 30-year veteran of the information security industry. I've worked as an entrepreneur, a consultant, and an analyst. I've helped a lot of start-ups to grow into prosperous companies, along with working on many enterprise strategies.

In recent years, I've focused on community-based efforts within information security. I was the executive director of the Information Systems Security Association in the mid-2000s. In 2009, I founded Cloud Security Alliance and I have served as its CEO ever since.

Cloud Security Alliance is a not-for-profit organization that's focused on studying and carrying out much of the fundamental consensus research around best practices for securing cloud computing. This involves understanding threats and how we can increase the security baseline of ecosystems.

The cloud is now reaching a level of maturity and experiencing widespread adoption, so we understand more about next-generation issues. This includes the nexus between the Internet of Things (IoT), blockchain, artificial intelligence (AI), and some other key trends and technologies such as cloud computing.

Information security is more about the journey than the destination. We now have thoughtful adversaries and new technology trends to deal with. It's important to look at how cloud computing, which is moving to the center of the industry, can evolve to secure the rest of the world, along with how it's going to need to harmonize with some of these other trends.

Shira Rubinoff: Can you explain the difference between the three types of services that we find in cloud computing: Software as a Service (SaaS), Platform as a Service (PaaS), and Infrastructure as a Service (IaaS)?

Jim Reavis: The fundamental definition of cloud computing came from the National Institute of Standards and Technology (NIST), which defined the essential characteristics and the deployment mode: private versus public. The delivery models are probably talked about most, however.

I'll start with IaaS. That's considered to be the physical aspects of data centers and computers all the way up to the operating systems and the hypervisor they're managing. IaaS is about virtualizing all this, as well as the necessary layer of APIs to make it accessible, usable, and managed by the other layers.

PaaS is inclusive of the IaaS layer. You add on the necessary APIs and development tools to allow for rapid development of applications in a way that abstracts some of the complexities and some of the areas of the infrastructure itself. This could be handling encryption, load balancing, geographical diversities, and so on. PaaS is something that can be abstracted out so the developer doesn't always need to know about it.

SaaS is the full business application that's inclusive of those other layers. SaaS has the essential characteristics of being elastic, multi-tenanted, and a product of shared resources. But actually, you are delivering a different capability with each of the three models.

Shira Rubinoff: Why is cybersecurity so complex in cloud technology?

Jim Reavis: When you have a basic move from computation as a utility to something that you buy and procure, it breaks some of the traditional models and thinking about how you secure computation; it becomes a much more obvious shared responsibility because you don't even have a single owner of the computation itself.

You might have a cloud provider that owns and configures the hardware itself and the operating system layers, but you might have completely different companies managing software by updating it, configuring other aspects of it, and moving the data to it. Shared responsibility is one of the biggest causes of complexity.

Another factor is the rapidity of change. In the traditional world, where we built a lot of our information security best practices, technology is updated infrequently. You might update a major operating system or a major application only a couple of times a year. With the cloud, the on-demand provisioning has led to continuous deployment. You actually change the technology and how it's configured and used many times a day. You may have a virtual machine or a container that does a task for a few seconds and then disappears.

This raises the bar in terms of understanding how to coordinate, log, and track things. We have to figure out how to use our security practices in a much more automated and rapid way. On the other hand, sometimes we have to create new practices out of the cloud. So, the shared model and the speed are the two areas that bring complexity to the cloud.

Shira Rubinoff: Would you say that knowing where data sits is one of the big challenges that organizations struggle with?

Jim Reavis: I distinguish between physically knowing where data is and knowing what the governing rules and laws are that may apply based on where that location is. You could make the case that even in traditional on-premise IT systems, you may have difficulty in pointing to where information may be located.

We've been moving to a more virtual, managed view of technology for quite some time. With the cloud, it becomes even easier to move information around between geographical locations or cloud provider availability zones. That does create issues.

I've seen this happen; an organization was looking to create redundancy in its systems and to find a way to do a hard backup. What the company did was put information into a different region where laws were actually applied differently. This created a violation of privacy data protection law. That's something that can happen because the cloud is very good at allowing you to make lots of copies while being very redundant in your information management. It ends up being harder to delete information.

In terms of data sovereignty, it's very hard to say with a degree of specificity what the governing laws are that they apply or tie specific cloud instances to physical geographic locations. You've got to understand exactly how you're going to configure your information.

Another issue is storage bucket mismanagement, where you have a new storage bucket with the major mainstream cloud infrastructure services and they are not connected to any type of network interface. They're not accessible. Sensitive information will get put into the storage bucket. Then, someone else within the organization may attach that information to the compute in the network in a way that is world-readable. They may even forget about it and think they decommissioned the storage bucket and it's still just floating out there in an orphaned way.

Shira Rubinoff: There are issues with the General Data Protection Regulation (GDPR) that's across Europe affecting the U.S. and Canada; do you think it can be applied in one fashion that will be accepted across the industry?

Jim Reavis: I'm doubtful about uniformity in terms of information privacy. I do think that GDPR is creating much more commonality. Some of our corporate members, which are very large, multinational organizations, have said it's easier for them to just standardize GDPR for how they handle information.

Regardless of whether we're talking about the European Union or not, it's just easier to have one standard and best practice. However, countries themselves are not going to be in agreement. There are a few big countries that will not use GDPR inside of their jurisdiction.

You have so many different sensitivities of information. Some things should be public and there is no risk, whereas some things are top secret. What I'm looking for is the implementation of better, more sophisticated technology. Encryption we've had for quite a while, but it's the implementation of very sophisticated types of key management paired with encryption that will actually support any number of data privacy laws. That's very achievable.

The technology itself has been invented; it just hasn't been deployed and agreed upon by the different stakeholders. Once that happens, we could create a virtual France within a Los Angeles data center, for example. Giving the right information to the right authorities is a matter of the chain of custody of keys and the laws that would govern this.

I think that most cloud providers want to follow the law, but they don't want to be involved in law enforcement if they don't have to be. It's really a matter of having technology that gives the data controller the capability to decide who has access to information. This gives them the right to comply with laws without an intermediate cloud provider needing to do that.

Shira Rubinoff: Can you talk a little bit about future IT and cloud trends, and their impact on security?

Jim Reavis: One thing that's certainly clear is that in information security, when you have a very thoughtful adversary that you are trying to protect information from—whether that is a nation-state or individual hacking group or criminal enterprise—it will continue to adapt and technology will continue to adapt.

We don't solve the information security problem definitively; we move it around and we have different heat spots that we need to address. The explosion of IoT devices and just the explosion of compute in general are creating a great risk of losing privacy in a very broad sense and also just losing control of managing systems.

What we see as being fundamental to protecting that is a leap in the capabilities of machine learning. I'm not talking about AI as much as I was a couple of years ago; it's not lived up yet to the promise applied specifically to information security.

We need to create scale to help with automation. Machine learning is important because when done right, we can actually gain better control over our IT systems. DevOps, continuous deployment, continuous integration, and information security being able to shift left would create a lot of promise—from the backend perspective—for being able to better secure and really engineer our security versus it being something that is crafted in a server as a one-off.

With blockchain, we can take away the cryptocurrency aspect of it and just focus on the immutable ledger aspect to what it does. Some people see blockchain as the anti-cloud and believe that we're going back to this distributed view of the world in a new way.

I actually think that blockchain, when merged and integrated thoughtfully with cloud computing, is going to be one of the most significant things in the next 15 years. Blockchain will create new models for how to make information completely opaque to cloud providers, the bad guys, and other people in the technology chain who you actually don't want to have access to the information. Blockchain could return the control of information back to individuals or any business itself. That's an area we're focusing on.

Blockchain will provide a lot of the rules and the evidence about how systems are audited, how systems are changed, who has control of which assets, and when and why. Combined with encryption and everything else, that gives us hope.

If we combine AI, blockchain, DevOps, and better integration of the IoT and the cloud, we're going to see more automated solutions or self-driving cybersecurity. We'll still have people, but they're going to be monitoring more closed-loop systems and brainstorming how to actually use these capabilities for the good of humanity versus just looking at every bit and byte that goes by. I see the cloud as being at the center of that. That's going to be the deployment leverage point for taking security to the rest of the world.

Shira Rubinoff: Do you think there's any specific sector that's taking the lead on digital transformation in the cloud or even pushing towards the cloud with blockchain?

Jim Reavis: Yes, the more regulated industries or financial services are because they have more money to spend. I have seen some very interesting things happening. More specifically, in the financial technology area, there is a combination of high resilience/high security and entrepreneurs working in that area. That is leading to a blending of different trends in order to look at doing security in new ways.

Shira Rubinoff: Do you have any last thoughts around cloud computing/ cloud security?

Jim Reavis: What we've seen from analysts is that cloud computing is now the default IT system and it's surpassed traditional on-premise IT in terms of the actual financial spend. We're going to see much more adoption. There's now a great opportunity for information security to get rid of some legacy approaches and do them better.

Shira Rubinoff: Thank you, Jim Reavis.

Discussion

As companies migrate to the cloud, this new paradigm adds complexity when it comes to cybersecurity. Akin to many technological advancements, old problems are solved and new problems are created.

Cloud security

The move to the cloud changes the rules of the game. In the past, there was one point of entry to nearly any system. If we fast-forward to today, the concept of work has changed and is geographically dispersed. As discussed, we have shifted to data-centric security instead of an infrastructure-centric security model. The protocol will travel with the data, as people have to be able to access the data without compromising security. This is the new normal in the age of cloud security.

I want to highlight the obvious takeaway from this chapter: the security of your organization's data within the cloud is still your organization's responsibility. It's critical to realize that when it comes to cloud security, the cloud provider secures the perimeter of the cloud, but the organization needs to be responsible for the data it holds within the cloud's perimeter. Too many organizations rely on the cloud provider to keep their data secure and don't properly encrypt the data within the cloud. You are never off the hook – the cloud doesn't absolve you of your responsibility.

You probably noticed that cybersecurity is a very complex element when dealing with cloud technology. As Jim sums up, by its very nature, security is a much more shared responsibility in cloud computing. There are multiple stakeholders including your company, the cloud computing provider, which owns and configures the cloud themselves, as well as third-party software companies that can often update and configuring aspects and even move data into their own systems.

Now we've established that while the cloud isn't yours, its security remains in your purview, how do you devise the most cost-effective way to protect data? The good news is that you don't have to re-invent the wheel, as the parameters around cloud security are clearly defined.

Kevin referred to the Cloud Control Matrix or CCM, which has been developed by Cloud Security Alliance, of which Jim Reavis is the CEO. The key philosophy behind CCM is that the controls cannot be static, and this is a pivotal concept that helps buttress your overall cyber hygiene.

Know your data

Knowing your data is basic and fundamental to your security posture in the age of cloud computing, yet many organizations skip over this crucial step. What this means is very simple: you need to know where your data sits, who has access to it, and the type of data it is.

Kevin recommends avoiding arbitrarily labeling data by the magnitude of sensitivity, as it isn't effective. Basic demographic attributes could put people's lives in danger in certain parts of the world, while in other areas it could be essential to effectively deliver goods and services. In sum, know your data, but don't apply random systems of designation as it will lead you nowhere.

It's important to mention that a monumental part of knowing your data is being cognizant of the nature of your data. As Kevin underscored with his example of legal contract data, the nature of the data dictates what rules and regulations are relevant to your organizational responsibilities. As time goes on, your responsibilities will change because of a shifting regulatory regime, and you have to know your data if you're interested in following the rules.

GDPR is great example of how important knowing your data is to keeping it safe and conforming to rules and regulations. The European framework ignited a trend of commonality and uniformity and many websites started telling people about the data being collected by cookies. Naturally, it's easier to have one standard and best practice when dealing with privacy.

Regulations such as GDPR will affect how long you should keep your data. Especially amidst a changing regulatory landscape, data storage should be a major consideration for your data management plan, whether its short-term, medium-term, or long-term. Be aware that storing it long-term could be a detriment to security, but you might need the data.

Additionally, storing it when you don't need to store it can cause all sorts of problems; if and when a breach occurs, data that wasn't necessary to your organization can still be very valuable to bad actors when stolen, who can use it to cause significant harm to your customers.

Just like anything else, many countries will not be in agreement with one standard. That's why many North American companies are adopting a wait-and-see approach to GDPR and waiting to see if people get fined or it becomes the global standard. Cybersecurity in the cloud will continue to evolve as the regulatory regime advances and achieves global harmony.

Looking forward

When discussing future cloud trends and the impact of security, everyone is agreement regarding the importance of being both reactive and proactive in your security posture. When you're thinking about a forward-thinking adversary from whom you're trying to protect information, as Jim points out, it does not matter whether it is an individual, a hacking group or nation-state, or a criminal enterprise, the adversary will continue to adapt and technology will need to adapt as well.

As you're moving to the cloud, think of it as an opportunity to improve your cyber hygiene. The move to the cloud means that security can simultaneously be improved and get rid of the old standards of legacy approaches, as they have become outdated and as technology advances, our security needs to as well.

Summary

Cloud computing has changed the way millions of people manage their data, creating an unprecedented level of convenience in a cost-effective manner. At the same time, the move to the cloud has rewritten the rules of cybersecurity. In some ways, while cloud computing made data management easier, it has simultaneously become more difficult to know your data.

As governments around the world race to develop regulatory regimes around data, cloud computing will continue to create complexities for businesses.

In a globalized world, it's critical that industry groups be ahead of the curve and provide guidance for governmental bodies. Groups such as the Cloud Computing Alliance will prove to be indispensable in harmonizing baseline standards for organizations that work across countless jurisdictions and find themselves subject to a varying patchwork of regulations.

The onslaught of regulations is a direct response to the constant flow of breaches that we're seeing on a regular basis. In many cases, breaches that make international headlines force organizations to confront the shortfalls of their security posture. While governments, businesses, and consumers align in their desire to keep data safe and away from bad actors, many of the world's largest breaches occurred simply because of poor cyber hygiene.

In the next chapter, we're going to review what we can learn from the world's biggest breaches, and how proactive and reactive approaches to cybersecurity can help us navigate today's changing landscape. The biggest breaches in recent history can provide clear takeaways in what best practices at your organizations should be moving forward to keep your data safe.

5

The World's Biggest Data Breaches – Proactive and Reactive Approaches

As we discussed in the last chapter, the push to the cloud is a double-edged sword; it's not a cure-all for every one of your ongoing security issues. In fact, it can open a door to data breaches if not implemented and continuously monitored.

That's one vital lesson in a digital world where access to information is always at our fingertips. Technological progress solves old problems and creates new ones. Anyone who's watched the news or used the Internet during the past decade has likely learned of multiple major data breaches.

In fact, sometimes it seems like data breaches have become so common that they're shrugged off by many people, who dismiss any relevant news reports about breaches with a "here we go again" attitude. This attitude is a very dangerous one to have as something that becomes commonplace or the "norm" can yield behavior that's reactive, rather than proactive or sensitive to the potential of breaches occurring.

That said, there are a small number of breaches that stand apart from others as posing much greater risks to many more people than the typical breach. In this chapter, I'll look at major breaches and the organizations that they target, as well as the scale of data affected. Additionally, I'll discuss how to best reduce the likelihood of such breaches occurring in the future, as well as how to address them if and when they do occur.

Tom Kellermann

Tom Kellermann is the Chief Cybersecurity Officer for Carbon Black Inc. Prior to joining Carbon Black, Tom was the CEO and founder of Strategic Cyber Ventures and was appointed the Wilson Center's Global Fellow for Cyber Policy in 2017.

Shira Rubinoff: Why do we keep hearing about data breaches in the news? The practice of information security in the realm of digital data has been around for decades. Why do we still have such a problem?

Tom Kellermann: There's a handful of reasons why this is occurring: firstly, you see more of an arms bazaar of attack capabilities that are widely available to cyber criminals, allowing them to bypass traditional cybersecurity capabilities, like firewalls, encryption, and antivirus software.

Secondly, much of the time—over 50% of the time, according to Carbon Black—we're seeing adversaries conduct what's called island hopping. Essentially, they target an organization and then from that organization's network, they target the customers, partners, and/or government agencies that are relying on the information flow from that organization. Lateral movement through island hopping creates a kind of contagion across entire industries.

Thirdly, most organizations do not conduct threat-hunting exercises and thus are not aware when they have been compromised. It usually takes around 100 days for an organization to realize that it's been breached and as a result, you have these adversaries, criminals, and spies dwelling on systems and infrastructures at their own leisure until they do something that's a little bit too noisy.

Finally, technological advances and the migration to low mobility, software applications, and cloud computing have really undermined the security architectures that have been espoused by the standards bodies and kind of thrown them on their head. It's far too easy now to bypass the perimeter and the security of an organization because of those technological transformations.

Shira Rubinoff: In your opinion, which data breaches have been the most significant to date; why do you consider them to be the most significant; and what lessons can be learned from them?

Tom Kellermann: The most significant data breach to date is the one that in 2017 pilfered the U.S. Government's cyber armory and allowed for those cyber weapons to go onto the streets of the dark web. That was the Vault 7 breach.

I think that recently, there have been some other very significant breaches. There was the 2018 compromise of Marriott and the impact that had on literally about one-third of the world's business travelers. This was compounded by the fact that passport information was stolen and it looked like the Chinese were in those systems, because they were competing with Marriott for the acquisition of Starwood. They were using their footprint even after they lost the bid, to conduct espionage on business travelers around the world. That's highly problematic.

I also think that the 2018 Docker breach is quite significant because of the way in which application developers were using Docker and the ecosystem to create applications. The systemic nature of that breach, and how that could impact the greater technology ecosystem, was quite profound.

Then, you have the major significant breaches that we all know about but that set the bar for destructive attacks, like the 2017 Russian NotPetya attacks against Ukraine, which leveraged a destructive polymorphic worm into systems. That signaled a turning point towards dramatic escalation in cyberspace.

Carbon Black research noted that there was a 220% increase in destructive attacks this past summer and that actually, one in three breaches involved destruction—arson, essentially—of infrastructures by adversaries. That's quite troubling.

Shira Rubinoff: Obviously there were many information security countermeasures in place when those breaches happened. What technologies have emerged that can best help to prevent breaches and mega-breaches? If you're not satisfied with the current crop of offerings, what needs to emerge?

Tom Kellermann: I think endpoint security needs to be modernized as a whole because the endpoint is the beginning and end of most breaches. Network security capabilities are failing in large part because the network itself has become so ephemeral.

The hunt capabilities and the EDR capabilities that are out there are incredibly useful if you regularly use them to capture all unfiltered data, and to conduct continuous monitoring. I think deception technology is here to stay, which at least gives you zero false positives on attack paths that can be triggered by adversaries.

Robust, next-generation authentication capabilities are very important, as are the capabilities that allow you to limit privileged access and to actually assess when privileges have been increased as the superusers are created throughout an environment, and forcibly turn those superuser privileges off. That's one of the first things adversaries do: they actually ask for the privileges and compromise credentials.

I also think memory augmentation applied to security operation centers is incredibly useful. Because of the way we're migrating to cloud computing, creating secure containers and container security is very important as well.

Shira Rubinoff: What trends have you observed over the past few years surrounding attacks that have succeeded and led to breaches?

Tom Kellermann: From an attack-factor perspective, they've leveraged a lot of fileless malware through email and through applications.

There is a much stronger counter-incident response, with the adversaries actually reacting to the defender now, as the adversary is not just attempting to conduct a burglary per se: they're actually conducting home invasions. They're not only deleting logs, but disabling Windows Defender and network security capabilities.

We're seeing an increase in the use of worms again. We used to see these in the past but now they are resurging, especially IoT-enabled worms. Even vapor worms, which are worms that empower the distribution of fileless malware.

There's much more living off the land. The adversaries are using trusted protocols and communications channels that are implicitly allowed within organizations against the organizations themselves.

Shira Rubinoff: How have privacy regulations impacted data breaches and protected against breaches, for example, HIPAA, GDPR, or GLBA?

Tom Kellermann: Those are different animals. I don't think you can make a distinction between privacy and cybersecurity. I don't think you can actually have privacy without cybersecurity.

There isn't one Big Brother. I think that there are many governments out there that operate as Big Brothers in the Orwellian concept, as well as many non-state actor groups that have the technical self-welfare to be omniscient and telepathic.

The most proactive regulations out there outside of GDPR are the Monetary Authority of Singapore's banking security regulations, called the Technology Risk Management Guidelines. I do think that hopefully, with the new U.S. Congress coming in, we will see a federal data-breach law enacted to get over the state-by-state requirements. I'm very concerned that domestically in the U.S., the state-by-state regulations on data breaches state that you don't have to report them as long as the data was encrypted.

You and I both know that if I compromise the credentials of someone on an endpoint level or server level, I can unlock any encryption. So, what good is it to say you don't have to report because the data was encrypted? The data at rest and the data at use can still be accessed by someone owning that endpoint. So, that has to change.

In addition to that, the European mandate is that within 72 hours of a breach, companies have to report it. As much as that's proactive and good, the challenge there is that many organizations may choose not to conduct threat-hunting exercises or penetration tests, or become more proactive with their cybersecurity because they can always hide behind a veil of plausible deniability.

Why would I try to improve my visibility and continuous monitoring if, all of a sudden, when triggered, I have to immediately go into crisis communications mode?

I think GDPR is a great step in the right direction. I'm hoping that this U.S. Congress does something proactive. Given that every member of the U.S. Congress was impacted by the Marriott breach in some way, shape, or form, I do think that will be the tipping point and the catalyst for change.

Shira Rubinoff: You actually touched upon my next question: can elected officials help? Are they the solution, or are they really part of the problem?

Tom Kellermann: Beyond that, I think that the U.S. Government should empower the Department of Homeland Security to help critical infrastructures in a greater fashion to secure their systems.

Electoral systems should be defined as critical infrastructure, and they should be forced to a higher standard—a federal standard—for security. A RICO statute should be applied to cybercrime and there are a number of things that can be done, not all of which require new legislation. A more proactive and modern approach to the nature of organized crime is needed.

Keep in mind also that the Russians have been successful in defeating the U.S. and U.K. cyber defenses due to the fact that the cybersecurity architectures are obsolete; they were built to defend against the kill-chain. The Russians' attack matrix is not a kill-chain. Rather, it is a Cognitive Attack Loop (CAL) as evidenced by the surge of counter-incident response, island hopping, and destructive attacks. This has allowed them to stoke a cyber-insurgency in American cyberspace. In order to wage the counter-insurgency we must spin the chess board and disrupt the CAL. The kill-chain is obsolete – we must measure success by disruption of attacker behavior. Understanding root cause is paramount. Combination of TTPs define intent.

Shira Rubinoff: Do you have any good war stories from performing forensic analysis after a breach?

Tom Kellermann: The interesting thing about Carbon Black, and the reason why I joined the company, is that our hunt capability is involved in two-thirds of the world's cybercrime investigations.

Given that, we started asking our major IR partners from Kroll to Optiv, to RedCanary, and so on, what they're seeing out there. I think the way you're seeing the human on the other side of the keyboard reacting to the defender in today's world is quite troubling.

It's not just the deletion of logs, but the actual destruction of subnets of data. The integrity attack phenomenon, where the attack is changing the value of data, or the time associated with data, has become quite problematic, especially in financial sectors. That's something I think we're going to see an increase of.

Also, the Chinese—through the Cloud Hopper campaign—have been leveraging very elegant attacks, where they've been targeting the managed security service providers through their cloud infrastructure and then from that, they're island hopping into their major corporate clients. Once they steal what they want from the strategic plans, or the intellectual cybercrime investigations property of those major corporations, they then turn those corporate websites into watering holes. I've never seen such overt cyber colonization before, but that's what's been going on over the last 10 months.

Shira Rubinoff: Is there any story specifically that you would say sticks out more than the others?

Tom Kellermann: Yes, there is a story about Belan and Bogachev, two of the original digital dogs of Silicon Valley and of the dark web in St. Petersburg. They transitioned from bank heists to cyber bank heists, to becoming cyber militia members for Vladimir Putin.

I thought it was quite fascinating to watch them and their crews become less active in 2015 and '16 against financial institutions, and become more active towards targeting Western and NATO targets. The hack of the 2016 election is just the tip of the iceberg.

The most interesting breach that I saw was associated with the Pawn Storm campaign identified by Trend Micro when I was there. That was when the 2,300 most powerful people in Washington D.C. and New York had their cell phones and mobile devices compromised, as well as their spouses' and their lovers' information.

That was accomplished with a very unique payload that allowed for the use of proximity settings that could leverage emissions to physical environments. They could pop the microphones and cameras specific to location settings, and take recordings that could then be digitized. That was quite prolific and what they call in Washington D.C. a "button-down": when you have compromising information on someone that makes them vulnerable to extortion.

Shira Rubinoff: What are the problems today in how businesses are organized in terms of structure and where the responsibility falls should a breach occur?

Tom Kellermann: There's a governance crisis currently in American cybersecurity. I'm hoping that the data protection officer mandated by the European Union's General Data Protection Regulation (GDPR) becomes someone who's more than just a legal mind, and that this could become the career path of choice for CISOs.

Frankly, Chief Information Officers (CIOs) are pretty much like financial officers. They're focused on managing resources, increasing efficiencies, and increasing access. As a result, they're increasing the attack surface.

I would hope that we will start seeing security as a functionality in conducting business and truly dealing with security like we would safety. We need to understand that the digital safety of not just our organization but our customers is at stake.

One thing that people always forget is the following: the worst thing to happen from a data breach is not the theft of data, the destruction of data, or the denial of service; it's your organization's digital identity being used to attack other organizations. That's the worst-case scenario.

That island-hopping phenomenon is highly problematic and can dramatically impact not just the reputation of an organization and a brand, but the lawsuits that will come, someday, as a result of criminal negligence on behalf of organizations who have failed to properly secure their infrastructure. The impact of that will be astounding.

Shira Rubinoff: Is there anything else you'd like to add around the topic of data breaches that I didn't touch upon?

Tom Kellermann: The way that we currently conduct incident response is outdated. Incident response must evolve. It must become more proactive; not just by regularly conducting hunt exercises, but by IR teams conducting penetration tests from the perspective of the compromised devices and hosts to understand the true attack path that could be leveraged from their infrastructure to the outside world.

These paths don't just show them how the data could have been exfiltrated but, more importantly, how the adversary could move laterally through their network against others. I do think that authentication is truly the Achilles' heel of cybersecurity. Multi-factor authentication is still insufficient. We need to really get to two- and three-factor authentication. We need to actually conduct liveness tests and challenge the responses of individuals when they access systems. We must be able to toggle authentication up and down, specific to the level of risk not just to the network, but to the individual and/or from the context around where the individual has been, both physically and digitally, in the past.

Due to current ineffective U.S. diplomacy, we are beginning to see a manifestation that is unprecedented in the history of the U.S. by our adversaries in cyberspace. I do feel that as relations with Russia and China deteriorate—and they will continue to deteriorate—we're going to see a greater manifestation of cyber insurgency within the U.S. cyberspace. 2020's going to be a very dark year and I'm sorry to say that. I've been in the industry for 22 years now, and I am at a loss; not only about what is possible, but about how willing and able our Cold War adversaries are, at this place in history, to leverage soft power through cyber.

Shira Rubinoff: What do you think leads companies to have this false sense of security that if they put certain factors in place, they're secure and they can just continue as is? Certainly, these companies have great leadership, and understand security and privacy, yet some just continue to not make changes.

Tom Kellermann: I would hope that the American consumer, and corporations in general, choose to be discerning about who they do business with based on how seriously they take security.

That being said, I think that the issue is that security is invisible. As long as the technology is working, people don't really see a problem. The mythology behind encryption has allowed for many people to maintain plausible deniability or just live in denial, frankly. In my view, this will be the year that changes, and I think the Marriott breach is going to be the tipping point.

Shira Rubinoff: Thank you, Tom Kellermann.

My next discussion is with someone else I consider a thought leader in the space, who also happens to be a friend and a mentor to me. She'll lay out the current landscape and how through her career, she's become an expert in mitigating risk and identifying key takeaways to keep your organization safe.

Mary Ann Davidson

Mary Ann Davidson is the chief security officer (CSO) at Oracle, responsible for Oracle software security assurance. She serves on the international board of the Information Systems Security Association (ISSA), has been named one of Information Security's top five "Women of Vision," is a Federal 100 Award recipient from Federal Computer Week, and was recently named to the ISSA Hall of Fame.

Shira Rubinoff: Could you start by talking about what you're doing now?

Mary Ann Davidson: I'm the chief security officer for Oracle Corporation. Specifically, my area of responsibility is what I would call secure engineering or assurance. My team makes sure that everything that we build, including hardware, software, and anything that goes out of our company with an Oracle label on it, is built securely and maintained securely.

I have wonderful colleagues who handle all the other areas of IT security and cloud security. I feel very fortunate because I've got a great team. You're only as good as the people who are willing to work for you and with you.

Our executive management team really understands how important security is.

Shira Rubinoff: What is your background?

Mary Ann Davidson: I got an engineering degree, then I was a naval officer for several years. I was on active duty doing construction management and then served in a reserve naval construction battalion. After that, I got a master's in business and went to work in Silicon Valley.

I started off doing boring finance jobs. I ended up getting fired from the last finance job, which turned out to be a blessing because I wasn't good at it. An unusual series of circumstances led me to get a job at Oracle. I always say that God has a sense of humor because I've never liked computers!

That was my least favorite class when I was in college and I didn't like programming.

When I started working for Oracle, I just really liked my role. It was fun and there was a great work environment. Oracle was building up a new division at the time. I might sound boring when I say that I've been with the same company for such a long time, but Oracle is not the same company now as it was back then. I've been able to keep developing along with the company. I've also been very fortunate to have had opportunities that, in some cases, I wasn't really looking for.

Shira Rubinoff: What was your experience of being a naval officer?

Mary Ann Davidson: I'm happy that I had that experience. I always tell people that I learned everything I know about leadership in the military. The military teaches you how to lead well because you are asking people to, in some cases, actually put their lives on the line.

Shira Rubinoff: Data breaches are an important topic in the area of security and technology. What can organizations do to mitigate the risk?

Mary Ann Davidson: Nobody's perfect when it comes to running a network, but some actions are very basic. You'd be surprised at how many companies don't have a good asset inventory.

Somebody sticks up a server, then they forget about it and they don't patch it. I've heard of this happening after various viruses went around. A server wasn't patched or maintained and that was an entrée into an organization.

Staying on top of patching is critical. And it's sensible to do a risk assessment and identify what the most important assets are that need to be protected the fastest.

There are technologies that can help to protect your data. For example, you can fully encrypt your data. That makes it harder for somebody to walk off with information. In cases where somebody has to access data, such as if a new system needs testing with live-ish data, you don't necessarily want those testers to get access to key corporate data.

You can do data masking or data redaction, which means you give somebody something that looks like a valid social security number, but it really isn't. Sometimes you give a tester just enough data to use but not the pieces that are sensitive. Part of that process involves being able to trawl through your network to find sensitive pieces of data.

There isn't one magic bullet that's going to make your company perfectly secure. What you can do is create a discipline around how you approach securing your assets. Where are those assets? Who owns them? What are the things you need to keep patched?

Using the technologies that are available to protect data at rest and in transit doesn't mean that there will never be a data breach, but it's going to be much harder for a breach to be meaningful if the data is all encrypted, for example.

Shira Rubinoff: I think the big thing that companies struggle with is how to deal with hackers. Knowing where data sits is critical for every organization. How can organizations get a better handle on their sensitive data?

Mary Ann Davidson: There are tools available that will do data discovery for you. These tools will go through your systems and help you to find where sensitive data is. However, that's not always foolproof.

Most people are data hoarders. There are TV shows about people who hoard in their own homes, but, in a way, companies are like that too. Storage is pretty cheap now. You have these powerful systems, which means you can collect every piece of data and keep it as long as you want. There's this attitude of keeping data because you might need it someday.

You need to start questioning whether you actually need to keep data. If you keep it, you have to know how valuable it is and you have to protect it. This is the case especially now that we have the European General Data Protection Regulation (GDPR) and other privacy laws that specifically limit data retention.

I'm not saying data is bad; data is very powerful. I do think companies need to rethink why they have data and how long they keep it for. Companies also need to weigh up the risks of storing data. Storage isn't the same thing as using data; obviously, that's a business benefit.

I hope that regulations like GDPR will force companies to assess their data so they collect and retain just the data they need. With less data, there's also less information to protect. It's a balancing act, but data that's just sitting around is a target. Why collect and keep that data if it's not being used?

Shira Rubinoff: Do you have an example about the mishandling or misuse of data leading to a massive breach?

Mary Ann Davidson: This one example wasn't a massive breach, but it was a head-slap moment. This was in the days before bundled patches were the norm. Now, many organizations provide bundled security patches that come out quarterly because that works better for customers. In the old days, we would put one-off security patches out on an unpredictable schedule.

One company we were working with revealed that it had not patched its *most* critical system at all. This company was in a regulated industry, so doing this was critical. The company wanted to know whether it was at risk. It had received 67 security alerts and hadn't applied any of those patches.

The company was also using a version of a product that was no longer supported. When de-support notices are sent, it is critical that companies take action.

Bundling patches has helped and now there's technology available where you can patch things while they're still running, like in-memory patching. That's helpful because companies want to be protected, but they need to minimize having to take systems down or offline to be able to patch them.

Shira Rubinoff: Some people say that when the patches come through, they also have to check that the patching is going to work for their company's system. Instead of just applying a patch, they have to test it first. Is that something that you see clients worrying about?

Mary Ann Davidson: Yes, they want to make sure that they're not going to break something. Most vendors have tried to do a lot of this testing in advance, but that doesn't mean some customers won't still need to do some testing.

Shira Rubinoff: Let's move on to the topic of the cloud and cloud security. What does the move to the cloud do for security in your opinion?

Mary Ann Davidson: In general, I think that the cloud makes security better. Companies are now moving to the cloud because they think the security is better than what they could provide themselves.

That makes sense on the face of it. Let's say you're a cloud provider with 400 customers. Each customer has to test and integrate their own patches, for example. If you as a cloud provider can do this using an automated process, that's going to save each customer a fair amount of resources.

The general move to the cloud can also be understood from the standpoint of it being really hard to find security people. This is particularly true for small and medium enterprises. If a company's core competency isn't running systems, it's going to let somebody else run those systems. This frees the company up to use its resources for innovation.

A larger supplier or a larger service provider is likely to have access to more cybersecurity talent. Having a small number of people using automated tools to secure things makes more sense than every company having to go and find security experts. That doesn't scale very well.

There are some nuances here. For example, there are lots of different types of cloud use. There's the type where the service provider is running everything for the customer. The other type is where the customer is actually building its own systems but doesn't want to worry about the infrastructure part. The customer is building applications, but they're running on somebody else's Infrastructure as a Service or Platform as a Service.

That second case leads to a split in security responsibilities between the service provider and the customer. One thing that has to be very clear for any service provider is what it has responsibility for and what the customer has responsibility for. This is like when you rent an apartment. You're not maintaining the stuff in the building, but obviously, you're responsible for vacuuming your own apartment. Responsibilities need to be clear on both sides.

Shira Rubinoff: Do you think the movement to the cloud actually helps to mitigate data breaches?

Mary Ann Davidson: Yes, on a generic level. A cloud provider that already has the capability to do full data encryption may just provide that as part of the service. They may also do patching better and faster than their customers.

Where cloud becomes a challenge is where you have people in an enterprise who are using services that have not been given the blessing of the company. That can lead to data breaches. Employees may not understand what their responsibilities are and what the risks are.

You could share a document and somebody else could access it. That doesn't mean it's a good idea to do that with the corporate merger and acquisition plan. You may not have put the right access controls on it. Now you've got a very sensitive document that is no longer within your enterprise's control.

It's incumbent upon companies to have policies about what staff can and cannot use, and what kind of approvals they need. And these policies need to be enforced.

I don't think most employees are willfully trying to leak company secrets and get them on the front page of *The Wall Street Journal*. I just think people don't understand what the limits are or what the corporate concerns are about using some of these services that could, potentially, lead to a breach.

Shira Rubinoff: What are the key steps that companies should take when thinking about strengthening cyber hygiene and becoming less susceptible to a data breach?

Mary Ann Davidson: To take a step back, security is a discipline. Right after Christmas, you always see these adverts for diets. You might lose the weight initially, but you can only keep it off through a lifestyle change.

With security, you need to make long-term changes too. If you don't have a culture of security in your organization, there's no security pixie dust that's going to fix everything. That doesn't mean that every single person in your organization needs to be an IT security expert, but that culture needs to be there.

To go back to the points we talked about earlier, you need to be asking certain questions. What are our assets? Do we have asset owners? Do we have a good risk-based system? Do we have appropriate policies? If you don't make this part of the company culture, there will be problems.

The marines have an ethos that every marine is a rifleman. Every one of them goes through the same basic training. If somebody attacks them, you'll never hear a marine say, "Excuse me, Mr. Bad Guy, I'm just the administrative clerk." Again, not every one of us needs to be a marine, but that strong warrior culture is important. If you don't have a strong security culture, you're going to fail.

Shira Rubinoff: That's certainly sage advice. As a recognized and accomplished security executive, what career advice would you give to anyone who wants a job in security?

Mary Ann Davidson: You have to know who you are and be comfortable in yourself. The world is really hungry for integrity. You have the responsibility to promote security, as does everybody in your organization.

I always tell my team that they should give their best professional advice. If you don't work in an organization where you feel that you can give your professional opinion and have it heard, you've got to find another job.

Shira Rubinoff: Would you say that if colleagues are asking your opinion, they don't want you to just agree with them?

Mary Ann Davidson: Yes, and giving your opinion doesn't mean that you aren't prepared to be wrong. I've been wrong plenty of times. I encourage my team to challenge me. If you don't work in that kind of environment, you're going to be limited.

If managers hire clones of themselves, they're magnifying their own worst tendencies. Diversity means getting the best people you can. Ignore everything that has nothing to do with someone's ability to do the job. Having a diversity of talent and of viewpoints is what's really important; companies make better decisions that way.

Shira Rubinoff: Thank you, Mary Ann Davidson.

Discussion

It's unfortunate but true—data breaches are occurring far more frequently than they should, and we should resist accepting them as an unavoidable part of daily life. My interviews with both Tom and Mary stress the cold hard reality that these breaches could have been entirely avoided if the right protocols had been in place. This is precisely why practicing proper cyber hygiene is essential to ensuring a truly cyber secure environment.

Committing to a combined security posture that adds proactive security assessment to reactive security protocols is what ensures the sustainability of your defensives. But you can never back down, as what worked to defend your data yesterday may not work tomorrow, and your previously iron-clad plans could succumb to a breach in the face of new technologies and tactics. Infiltration techniques are rapidly evolving, so companies must identify vulnerabilities in their own systems before breaches happen. Attacks are happening, and there are many vehicles by which they can happen. Ultimately, whether a company is successfully breached depends on whether it stands back and allows a breach to occur, or contains the damage as it unfolds.

As a reminder, the four steps that we covered in detail in *Chapter 1*, *Integrating Humans and Technology – Four Steps to Cyber Hygiene*, that should be at the front and center of ensuring cyber hygiene within your company in order to prevent attacks, are:

1. Training across the entire organization
2. Global awareness of patterns and developments that can evolve rapidly
3. Updating systems, such as OSs, for optimal patching and next-gen authentication
4. Implementing Zero Trust across organizations to limit access to sensitive data

Let's now break down these steps and explore them in the context of major data breaches.

Training across the entire organization

Living in a world rife with breaches means that education and training must be a priority within your organization. Present and future employees should be taught relevant practices and educated to develop the skills they need to address the litany of modern-day cyber dangers. This effort should be continuous, and adapt to the changing landscape. As technology and best practices advance, education and training must advance in tandem.

Let's not forget that the foundation of training and education should be an established protocol; a specific set of steps that needs to be followed post-breach for both security and personnel, to evaluate who has access to what information, the messaging that goes out, how it goes out, and when it goes out.

This established protocol will deploy both proactive measures—a very simple example might be regularly scheduled password changes—as well as reactive measures to contain breaches, such as requiring all employees to change passwords after a breach and the institution of new, stricter security protocols within the organization.

Mary Ann Davidson explained clearly that everyone in an organization is responsible for security. Your training and education initiatives should reflect the overarching goal of cyber hygiene. It's not just about cybersecurity professionals: everyone has skin in the game, including public relations managers, human resources officers, attorneys, and rank-and-file employees. Breaches are not problems that are confined to a certain subset of your organization—they are an organization-wide problem that requires organization-wide solutions.

Critically, management within the organization must understand that threats are real, and correspondingly, the team and the responsibilities and budgets need to be allocated appropriately across all departments in order to incentivize people to do their jobs and be proactive in fighting off future threats. Setting up systems within the organization should include the CISO and the CIO. The budgets should be separate but employees should also be encouraged to work together if need be.

The CISO, CIO, and the Chief Operating Officer (COO) should each have the tools and budgets to fulfill their respective duties independently, but at any point, they should be incentivized to better synchronize their efforts and work together to tackle a specific issue. This co-operation will trickle down through the entire organization, and training and education will cement the established processes in the event of a cyber incident.

Tom Kellerman underlines that being ahead of the curve is what protects you in the long run, especially as threats such as island hopping continue to threaten a wide range of entities nearly everywhere.

One of the scary trends that Tom alluded to is that attackers now react to defender actions and capabilities—they do a lot more planning and intelligence gathering about intended targets, learn from failed breach attempts, and act accordingly. Cybersecurity has, in that sense, become a true "cat versus mouse" type of battle, and this trend will only grow more pronounced as AI becomes more prevalent, creating an AI vs AI battle for cybersecurity supremacy.

This is just one example of how things have changed rapidly, and will continue to shift as time goes on. Organization-wide training empowers and builds the capacity to continually adapt to the changing nature of what it means to have proper cyber hygiene, including, as Tom mentioned, Conduct Incident Response. It is important to create a company culture focused on cyber hygiene across all parameters, including workflow and deliverables.

Global awareness of patterns and developments

Global awareness is a critical component as the world is more interconnected than ever. Before we get into how small the world has become, and how we need to be cognizant of evolving threat patterns on the other side of the globe, let's touch on a very important issue: we are in an age where we are becoming increasingly aware of the connection between governments and cyber adversaries.

There are varying opinions as how to respond to companies and how their respective countries of origin are becoming a major factor. I believe that consumers and corporations need to be careful about who they do business with, bearing in mind Tom's comment about how seriously these foreign companies take security. It has been well documented that a disproportionate amount of global cybercrime originates in China and Russia. Tom believes that as relations with these countries decline, we will see more cyber insurgency within global cyberspace.

That's why global awareness starts in our own backyard; we shouldn't discount the threats here at home. Global becomes local quickly in a hyperconnected world because there are a slew of bad actors and adversaries within our own companies and borders that may be incentivized by foreign governments to carry out such attacks.

On a different note, we should review how, in a globalized economy, government policies in countries on the other side of the world can greatly influence the way you do business. Consider Mary Ann's example of how cloud-based computing and GDPR may have created an environment in which we should take a second look at how much data should be saved.

As storage has become less and less expensive over time, individuals and organizations have begun to be—in Mary Ann's words—data hoarders. Think back 25 years ago to the era of 20 MB hard drives and 1.44 MB floppies. Most people did not store extraneous data because doing so was cumbersome, expensive, and required significant amounts of time to be dedicated to storing across multiple devices. Today, when one can buy a 10 TB drive for under 200 dollars, the storage of most types of data has become so inexpensive that there's little incentive to clean out unnecessary items.

The arrival of cloud-based storage has meant even more copies, and increasingly inexpensive cloud-based storage incentivizes people to put off deleting unnecessary information. They may even keep multiple copies of unnecessary information stored in various ways.

From a security standpoint, this has created within many homes and offices numerous copies of vast repositories of information, some of which are likely not as well protected as they should be.

GDPR and other privacy regulations might be a wake-up call to use the "delete" button once again. Storing sensitive data has now become a much bigger potential liability, so there's a strong incentive to get rid of data that an organization no longer needs. Ever-changing privacy regulations illuminate why global awareness of patterns and developments keep the rules for proper cyber hygiene in constant flux. We're often operating with rapidly changing regulations, and that will inevitably affect day-to-day workflow.

Global awareness is a constant exercise that must include developments ranging from mistakes that were made right in your office, breaches that occurred thousands of miles away, the proclamation of public policy by a legislative body on a different continent that affects your ability to do business, and much more.

No one ever said it was easy to prevent data breaches, and updating systems is frequently a monumental amount of work that is often mundane and taxing. Since most companies have been breached at some point, over a long enough timeline, whatever security posture you have in place will be tested until its weaknesses are found, and updating is essential.

Updating systems, such as OSs, for optimal patching and next-gen authentication

Let's talk about the basics that are often overlooked as you embark on a system-wide update or patching. As Mary Ann alludes to in her interview, many companies don't have a good asset inventory. For example, someone puts up a server, forgets about it, and stops patching it. This can lead to various viruses polluting the server, and that server becomes an entry point into your organization. Knowing your assets is pivotal to successful updating and patching. This is the information that's used for a risk assessment: what are the assets, where do they sit, who owns them, who's responsible for them, and what do you need to keep your systems patched?

You should know how many devices you have within the organization and understand that there could be third-party software on each of these devices. Each device may have different software depending on who's using it. Additionally, **Bring Your Own Device (BYOD)** trends have evolved and grown to the point where it is commonplace for BYOD to be the standard organization-wide. They may have their laptop, their personal phone, and their work phone. People download things to their personal devices on a regular basis. They may be accessing servers or running software on their own devices that do not adhere to the property security protocols you have in place. Even extreme measures like Wi-Fi blocking for personal devices doesn't work, because people still have cell phone signal. People can and will find ways around these measures and still work on their own devices. For instance, you can make your personal phone a hotspot. In a hyperconnected world, security protocols need to be updated. These realities should be reflected in your updating policy.

It's advisable to put through patches in test mode to see if the patch is actually going to run. Then, if there are no issues, you can put it live; but this a cumbersome, time-consuming, and costly endeavor that's not simple to do. That's one reason so many companies don't keep up with updating their patches.

Moving on to authentication, today's authentication processes are still severely deficient, as Tom mentioned, despite our knowing for about two decades that this was likely the case. Robust next-gen authentication capabilities are very important for your security posture.

The proliferation of SaaS software as well as cloud services means that authentication policies needs to evolve with the times. Many entities that should be using multi-factor authentication for various purposes don't do so, and even if they do plenty of multi-factor authentication systems suffer from inherent weaknesses.

For example, there are YouTube videos that show how to unlock someone's phone simply and easily, using a lifted fingerprint. Even so, many people protect their phones and all of the sensitive data on them with nothing more than fingerprints. Various facial scan-based authentication engines can be tricked by photographs or videos of people, and, from the fact that the most common passwords are still "123456" and "password", we know that password authentication still suffers from serious problems.

If people can fraudulently authenticate themselves as others, and thereby gain unauthorized access, data breaches are going to occur; criminals know that it's often easier to social engineer people and then log in as them rather than try the digital equivalent of breaking down the front door and disabling alarm systems.

There's no reason to believe that this trend is going to change any time soon. While new authentication systems are constantly being piloted, and some even embraced in the ecosystem, the systems that tend to become popular are typically those that suffer from weaknesses. The driver of adoption is usability, not security. The school of thought that creating authentication technology should have no extra steps for users has fallen flat in some ways, as some of these technologies have overlooked the necessity of accompanying ease of use with the security that's critical for the authentication to succeed. Smartphone passwords are replaced with fingerprint scans because it is more convenient, not because it is more secure.

Mary Ann discusses that cloud computing helps with data security because cloud providers already have the capability to perform full data encryption, and they may patch their software faster and more completely than their customers do. We must understand that the cloud provider secures the perimeter of the cloud, but the organization is responsible for securing their own data within the cloud. Some organizations don't pay attention to this responsibility and leave the data within the cloud unencrypted.

Implementing Zero Trust across organizations to limit access to sensitive data

Finally, restricting access by using a Zero Trust model cannot be overlooked, along with establishing trusted communication channels and protocols agreed upon by both upper management and the people who need access to sensitive data. You want an organization-wide standard, as both of my interviewees mentioned; implementing Zero Trust across the organization to limit access to sensitive data, unless access is granted per step, is a prudent and realistic measure.

We live in the age of Zero Trust, and there's no reason why your systems shouldn't reflect that reality.

In a Zero Trust system, access to data is only granted to the individuals who need access to that data. Each time a user requests information, that user must properly identify themselves to gain access to that information. By applying this every time, with no exceptions, this curtails a neglectful or malicious user's ability to move through an organization and "bucket-dump" information for current and later use. Heavy monitoring needs to be used on every step a user takes to access data, giving an organization better insight into its data and who accesses it.

This throws the need to delete data into sharp relief; data is the most sought-after asset a company has. It's what everyone is after. When companies store data that they don't need, they subject themselves to situations in which data can be lifted that should have never been stored in the first place. Even if we institute a Zero Trust model, people still have access to far more data than is appropriate, increasing risk for an asset that is extraneous and unnecessary.

Looking ahead

How is it possible to create safeguards for an ever-changing security landscape that evolves so quickly? The old way of reactive security may have been adequate for maintaining your security posture in the past, but today it's not nearly enough. Proactive security protocols and actions are essential in an ever-shifting world of cyber threats.

Our reality today is that a combined reactive and proactive security posture is imperative to remain secure as potential adversaries attack your organization. The next chapter lays out how every business has to evolve with the times, especially as connectivity reaches new heights that have never been seen before.

6

Trends in Cybersecurity

Welcome to the new world of cybersecurity, where hacks and breaches can no longer be completely prevented. It's not a matter of if, but a matter of when you're going to suffer a breach. In this environment, new systems that harness the power of cutting-edge technologies help us stay ahead of the curve and practice proper cyber hygiene.

The **Internet of Things (IoT)** is a prime example of how the challenges of cybersecurity are quickly becoming ever more challenging. IoT creates a world of unprecedented interconnectedness where every aspect of our businesses and our personal lives is connected to each other through a multitude of linked devices. Through these connections, we can glean a great deal of information to help us better navigate our daily challenges. Throw 5G into the mix, and we're talking about a world where communication is effortless, speedy, and convenient.

Unfortunately, linking everything is also creating unprecedented cybersecurity risks. Whenever you increase interconnectedness, you dramatically increase your system's entry points. If you imagine this phenomenon in a physical context, it's like trying to maintain a secure building while constantly adding entry and exit points—some of which you're unaware of. Naturally, this would be a daunting, if not impossible, task to carry out.

Tackling this brave new world of cybersecurity requires a rethink of the way we view organizational responsibilities, security versus efficiency, collaboration with industry peers, and the integration of new labor-saving technologies. Through my conversations with these two thought leaders in cybersecurity, we'll see how these trends in cybersecurity aren't only something to consider; they're central in today's ever more complicated world.

Barmak Meftah

Barmak Meftah is the President of AT&T Cybersecurity Solutions and CEO of AlienVault, an AT&T company. A veteran of the technology industry with a spectacular track record for delivering award-winning products, he's been passionate about building and leading great teams in enterprise software for over 20 years.

Shira Rubinoff: Could you talk about your background in the industry?

Barmak Meftah: I received my undergraduate and graduate degrees in computer science at the University of San Francisco. Since then, I've been in enterprise software.

I spent the early part of my career with Oracle Corporation. That was my initial exposure to enterprise software. I was running products for a couple of Oracle's mainline businesses: the relational database on the Windows platform and, for a short period of time, the application server. Then, I was introduced to Ted Schlein from Kleiner Perkins. He introduced me to Roger Thornton, whom I have worked alongside for many years.

In late 2003, early 2004, I was one of the early executives at Fortify Software, a company that was founded and incubated by Kleiner Perkins. Fortify Software was in the application security space. The company did extremely well and was bought by Hewlett Packard in 2010.

I ran the software security business at Hewlett Packard for about a year and four months until I joined AlienVault. AlienVault was a very small company that had moved its headquarters from Spain to the United States. I took over as chief executive officer (CEO) and president and brought with me a really strong team of executives from my time at Fortify Software, including Roger Thornton as our CTO who was one of the founders of Fortify.

AlienVault became a leader in unified security management, focusing on simplifying threat detection, security analytics, and incident response by integrating, automating, and orchestrating all of those technologies to work together. I talked to AT&T when the company expressed an interest in acquiring AlienVault. I found the idea of joining AT&T very exciting. I now serve as president of the cybersecurity business for AT&T Business.

Shira Rubinoff: The proliferation of IoT devices and technology is providing new and transformative opportunities, such as connecting everyday objects in order to collect and analyze data. What would you say are the biggest security risks associated with IoT and what can we do to mitigate those risks?

Barmak Meftah: I think the great thing about IoT is that we can connect pretty much everything. Through those connections, we can derive a lot of intelligence about how we live our lives.

Think about everything from your appliances at home to your car. Pretty much any object you interact with could potentially be a connected object. Combine that with the advent of 5G and there's going to be a new wave of communication that's based on extremely low latency, high throughput, and high speed.

Many of these embedded devices and embedded units can connect quickly, but the problem is the attack surface that this presents. The risks are very hard to quantify because they are unlike physical security risks. The easy part of physical security is that you typically understand the start and the finish of the perimeter that you're trying to defend. The problem with cybersecurity is that the perimeter is very amorphous, and it will only increase with IoT.

As we can't quantify the size, scale, start, or finish of these attack surfaces, the risks are going to dramatically increase because hackers will find new entry points into infrastructure.

Looking back to the 1960s or 1970s, attack surfaces were very limited as it was the days of the mainframe. Only two or three employees had access to the servers, so they were fairly protected. We went from that to client-server computing and open systems in the mid-1980s and early 1990s.

Suddenly, the attack surface for many companies increased because all internal employees had access to computers attached to the local area network. There was an explosion of insider threats.

Next, we moved to web services and the Internet. That meant that not just employees, but anything and anybody connected through a web browser could potentially be an attack surface or an entry point. With IoT, pretty much any connected device or any connected entity is now an attack surface.

IoT is a good thing, but as security professionals, we've got to start thinking about how we assess risk more effectively. How do we ultimately simplify the consumption of security products so that we can remove the seams or cracks that can be introduced by these expanding attack surfaces?

Shira Rubinoff: Could you give an example to illustrate what we just discussed?

Barmak Meftah: A great example would be autonomous cars. I'm actually sitting in my electric car right now. For a good majority of my drive, I had the car on autopilot and it was driving itself (of course, I was still paying attention to the road!)

The next wave is going to be fully autonomous cars. I actually suspect that this will become a reality over the next five years. As smart cities start to emerge, with traffic lights and stop signs all connected with IoT, these cars will begin to interact and be fully autonomous. We'll be able to input where we want to go into the navigation and the car will drive itself. This will change the way that we drive cars altogether.

We can, however, imagine the ramifications of a breach. In the past, the ramifications of a breach against a client-server computing environment were very limited. You could argue that even with the web, it was very limited. In the case of self-driving cars, however, a breach could actually cause accidents on a massive scale. We'd be dealing with human lives at risk. The consequences of making cars automated could be severe.

Shira Rubinoff: These kinds of cybersecurity trends are certainly at the forefront of many people's minds. Another important topic is the cybersecurity talent gap and the industry crisis surrounding that.

The demand for cybersecurity expertise will continue to rise as organizations realize that their current information security strategy is no longer sufficient. What do you feel is needed to address this problem?

Barmak Meftah: I think the economics of supply and demand will continue to be out of sync. Much of the innovation that's happening points to the need for more cybersecurity, especially if you look at the sheer number of companies that have come to the market over the last 10 years; there are thousands of security vendors and they all address very specific threat vectors.

It's important to emphasize or pay attention to producing more cybersecurity talent from educational institutions. The industry should also focus a little bit more on diversity. Cybersecurity has been a fairly male-dominated field for a long time. We need to find new ways of tackling cybersecurity and encourage more diversity.

In the meantime, I don't expect that the production of talent is going to exponentially increase to meet the supply and demand equation, so we just have to start looking more at automation. As an industry, we've focused too much on point products. We've inadvertently made the complex problem of security even more complex.

We need to reverse those trends and start thinking about how to make the consumption of security more automated, intelligent, integrated, and simple so that a company doesn't have to be encumbered with trying to glue together all of these point products. Companies need to use their scarce cybersecurity expertise and resources for higher-value services only.

Shira Rubinoff: Many people feel fearful that **artificial intelligence (AI)**, in combination with automation, will take away jobs. Others argue that automation will help with menial tasks but actually open the door for other types of positions too. What is your take on that?

Barmak Meftah: Given the scarcity of technology expertise, and especially cybersecurity expertise, I actually don't worry too much about automation replacing jobs. The demand for cybersecurity talent is a lot more than the supply that we have to offer, as we discussed.

If anything, automation will be used as a means of freeing up human capital resources so they can be used for higher-value services. I'm not too worried about a chief information security officer (CISO), for instance, saying that there are already too many people in an organization and automation can get rid of half of those people. Most CISOs realize that if they can automate and simplify their company's security blueprint, they can actually free up employees to start working on things that really require human intelligence and business context.

There's plenty of work to go around. If you talk to a typical CISO right now, they have more tasks and more initiatives than they have human capital resources. For the foreseeable future, AI, machine learning, automation, and integration are not going to put people out of jobs; they're going to replace the type of work that employees are doing, so they can then focus on higher-value work in the organization.

Shira Rubinoff: How do you feel we can better embed cybersecurity into companies?

Barmak Meftah: My former company, Fortify Software, believed that cybersecurity should be built into the fabric of IT assets. That will take away much of the extra work that we do to bolt security on after the fact. It's better to think about security during the assembly phase of the product.

If you talk to airplane manufacturers, for example, they don't let airplanes crash 100 times over and then start thinking about appropriate safety and security measures. Typically, issues around security and risk are thought through during the assembly process, so features can be built into the airplane.

When it comes to software—and even parts of hardware manufacturing—we must start thinking more about security during the software development life cycle, and the overall specification and assembly phase of an IT asset. Essentially, security should be built in rather than bolted on.

There's also a trend toward simplicity and consolidation. As an industry, we focus too much on inventing cybersecurity products that are very temporal in nature. The problem is that the threat cycle will continue evolving. There are going to be new threat vectors, new indicators of compromise, and new ways that hackers can gain access to an environment.

That cycle will be endless. The question becomes, how can we finally get to a point where we have predictive security? How can we actually be a step ahead of the hackers? In the game of cyber defense, the offenders have to be right only once and they can choose the timing of an attack. As defenders, we are at a distinct disadvantage where we have to be right all the time and we can't predict the timing of an attack. Because of this unfair equation, we must change the dynamics of the game and start focusing on areas of predictive risk and security.

Collaboration, sharing threat intelligence, crowdsourcing, and bringing together third-party security controls in an orchestrated and automated way will become key. We'll be able to take the task of gluing these third-party security controls together away from the end user.

Shira Rubinoff: A big topic that's being discussed right now is digital transformation within organizations. The problem is that the CISO has their set of rules, and the chief operating officer (COO) has theirs. Both parties are not incentivized to work together. What is your advice on moving away from seeing security as being just a check-the-box activity?

Barmak Meftah: When thinking about companies moving their assets from on-premises to the cloud, it is very rare that a company is 100 percent one or the other. Typically, companies operate in a hybrid environment where part of their computing and storage is on-premises and part of it is in the cloud. Having said that, there's absolutely no disputing that a massive digital transformation is happening and cloud-based deployments are on an exponential trajectory.

There are tremendous economic and technical advantages to cloud-based deployments. The problem, though, is that with digital transformation, the control that you thought you had over your IT assets is gone. Some of these IT assets, although they belong to you intellectually, are actually residing somewhere else. The way you think about security fundamentally has to change. There are new factors that you have to think about. Things are much more virtualized and software-defined, rather than physical and controllable.

Digital transformation will force thought processes to change. I think some of the interactions between the chief information officer (CIO), the CISO, the COO, and the chief financial officer (CFO) are going to change, as you mentioned, because risk and security are now becoming a board-level discussion, rather than being seen as just an IT element.

Until recently, CISOs fundamentally reported to CIOs. We're seeing a shift now to CISOs reporting to either chief risk officers (CROs) or directly to CEOs. CISOs might report to CIOs organizationally, but they now have a pretty firm seat in each board meeting. They give updates to the board in terms of the acceptability of risk, assessment of risk, and how the company should operate with other constraints. The more cybersecurity becomes a board-level agenda item, the more people are going to start to work together, rather than in isolated environments.

Shira Rubinoff: What do you see as being the biggest trends in cybersecurity for 2020 and 2021?

Barmak Meftah: We are already seeing more and more vendors talking about platforms, the unification of security, and the integration of security. Certainly, the advent of AI and machine learning points to trends of simplicity, integration, and automation, as we've discussed.

We will see a lot more innovation, research and development, and engineering dollars being spent on bringing together the appropriate set of security controls for a particular company, in a particular market segment.

This will allow for a software-defined virtualized platform that can change over time as the threat vectors change over time. How can we be as agile as the offenders? These hackers are extremely smart and collaborative. In response to that, we need to share threat intelligence more effectively.

If we continue to obsess over yet another security control that is very temporal, without paying attention to the automation and integration required to stay a step ahead of hackers, we'll be stuck in the same cycle. We need to make this complicated problem of security simple for companies of all sizes, from the smallest of SMBs to the largest of global enterprises.

Shira Rubinoff: You mentioned a number of times collaboration and sharing information. However, some very large companies may decide not to share the resources that gave them a leg up in the security industry. What would you say to that?

Barmak Meftah: A few years ago, we created an ecosystem of threat researchers and threat intelligence sharing called the **Open Threat Exchange (OTX)**. When we got started, we experienced some resistance from companies.

Now, the Open Threat Exchange has over 120,000 unique subscribers. We're sampling more than 20 million indicators of compromise every day. It's inevitable that crowdsourcing is going to overcome the select few companies that don't want to be involved. We're at the point where the majority of the industry agrees that sharing the appropriate threat intelligence is just good for all of us.

One thing that we were very stringent on when we launched the OTX was anonymizing the identity of companies and individuals contributing the threat data. You need to keep that confidentiality, but sharing threat data is going to grow to a point where everyone is doing it.

Shira Rubinoff: Are there any areas that you want to highlight that AT&T Cybersecurity is moving toward?

Barmak Meftah: One area we're focusing on is making threat intelligence actionable. To do that, we've created a threat intelligence unit called AT&T Alien Labs. It's a collaboration between AT&T threat researchers around the world, AT&T's unrivaled visibility of threat data on the Internet, our security researchers, and the threat intelligence of the OTX.

The second area of focus is making security very agile for the end user, so that it's possible to change the footprint of security on an ongoing basis as threat cycles evolve, without end users spending a lot of money on infrastructure.

The third area is predictive security. We want to point to early indicators of a security compromise in a predictive way so that our customers can see what's going to happen in the future and be proactive about it.

Shira Rubinoff: Are there any trends that you personally are really excited about?

Barmak Meftah: I always go back to automation. I've been in cybersecurity for almost 17 years. It's been this endless cycle of security controls. I'm very focused on just providing more integration, automation, and simplicity around the consumption of cybersecurity. It's time to take a step back and look at integration.

Shira Rubinoff: Thank you, Barmak Meftah.

Cleve Adams

Cleve Adams is a highly successful technology industry veteran who has been named one of the top 50 non-technical founders in tech industry history by The Huffington Post. A five-time CEO, Cleve has a flawless record of successfully managing companies on the cutting edge of tech from pre-revenue to valuations of over $1 billion for VC/PE firms.

Shira Rubinoff: Could you talk us through your background?

Cleve Adams: I went into technology right out of college. In 1997, I helped to start a company called Websense, which, along with Check Point and McAfee, was one of the first cybersecurity companies in the industry. I've been doing cybersecurity for companies ever since.

I've run four or five start-ups in cybersecurity, but right now, I'm CEO of Site 1001, a smart cities/buildings company. We develop AI software that makes buildings more responsive, efficient, and comfortable. Even though it's not specifically cybersecurity, there is a big cybersecurity component to our smart buildings.

Shira Rubinoff: What are the top trends in cybersecurity that we should expect to see in 2019 and beyond?

Cleve Adams: I think AI and machine learning really started to take hold in cybersecurity in 2019 and will be the dominant technologies in the industry going forward. Preventing cyber intrusions and hacks has always been a goal of cybersecurity, but the rate at which these attacks are evolving has made it very difficult for traditional cybersecurity systems to do that. AI is now reaching the point where it's sophisticated enough to start anticipating new attack vectors and adapt its own behavior to prevent them. As such, I think AI-powered, adaptive cybersecurity will completely replace older reactive systems within the next few years.

Shira Rubinoff: How has cybersecurity evolved during your time in the industry?

Cleve Adams: Back in the 1980s, mainframes dominated the industry. I worked for a little company called Novell, which developed NetWare, one of the first systems for linking personal computers into a shared network. With NetWare, suddenly you had networks of servers and PCs distributed all over, creating a need for both desktop computer and network security. Back then, because these computers weren't accessible to the outside world, most of the security tools then focused on securing physical access to the systems with passwords, and identity and access controls.

In the early '90s, the Internet came along, and all these networks that had been created with no concept of a global network were exposed to the whole world, posing a great problem for people in security. How could they secure their company, now that it had a network with many different devices all connected to this new thing called the Internet?

Many companies came up with ideas to try to solve this big problem. Companies such as Cisco were among the first to introduce firewalls to secure networks from outside intruders.

That was pretty good for a while, because people didn't understand how to get through firewalls or hack them. But because the Internet made it possible to install software without physical access to the machine, we started seeing malicious remotely installed software, aka "viruses," because there were a lot of people out there who wanted to bring down corporate networks and get at corporate information.

After that, crude content came into the workplace via the Internet, and that was often used as a payload for malware—security had to get tighter and stronger, so content filtering and security came on the scene. There were multi-layers of security: content filtering, content security, web security, and virus protection. Then came smartphones, tablets and Internet-connected everything and it got even more complex.

Now, it's a multi-layered industry with thousands of companies all competing and attempting to deliver the "next big thing" in a cybersecurity industry that's far more complex than it used to be.

Back in the early days, there were only a handful of us: Cisco, Check Point, McAfee, and Websense. Microsoft started getting into security as well and we partnered together to make things happen. It was a big partnership back then. We all shared our customers and our channels. That was a great time for security.

Shira Rubinoff: Today, many people are trying to share information about how to keep companies secure. You mentioned that you all partnered back in the early days, which I believe is the best way to go about security. However, some companies have taken the stance that they can be more cybersecure by not sharing information. What would you say about this approach?

Cleve Adams: If some traumatic event happens in your life or your company, things tighten up. You don't want people to enter your life or enter your company. You don't want to disclose information or talk about things that happen. This means that you tend to grow inward.

Companies tend to keep things to themselves because they think that's the most secure approach. When you get out and talk about breaches, that takes the power away from the hackers. It's valuable for companies to say that they got hacked, share how they overcame that, and suggest the tools that they used.

As time has gone on, more companies have realized that they aren't alone. There's much more sharing of information. Most executives out there today would agree that you can't win the battle by yourself. You have to partner up with different companies and go about security as a team, or as a village, so to speak.

Shira Rubinoff: Within organizations, we talk a lot about digital transformation, which involves the chief operating officer (COO) dealing with the chief information officer (CIO). You have to run the company and deal with cybersecurity at the same time. What would you say to companies about operations and security working together to be more cybersecure?

Cleve Adams: You just have to do it. COOs and CIOs often butt heads because they believe there's a trade-off between efficiency and security, but that's just not the case.

In this day and age, you can't have a profitable business without good cybersecurity, and there's no point in cybersecurity if the business is dying and has nothing to protect. Yes, there is some inconvenience on both sides, but it's worth it. You have to pay the price one way or another.

CIOs need to work with COOs, who need to work with the new CISOs today. CISOs need to be in place. They need to have an active role in the management of the company and the security of the company. CIOs are great when it comes to basic information, but when you need secure information, then the CISO needs to be the person who steps up and puts the security measures in place.

At Site 1001, we're going through similar issues. We're a small company that's growing very fast and we need to make sure that our networks, laptops, and edge devices are secure. Now that 5G is coming along, it makes everything a little more dangerous and mystical. So, we have to be up to speed on security measures.

Some companies won't do business with you unless you have in-house security protocols. This means that you need to be able to answer questions about how secure your company and data is: "Why would I install your technology in my company? How secure is your technology? Now that I'm selling my products into another company, how secure am I?" Companies need to answer those questions and they're being very diligent about doing just that.

Shira Rubinoff: Times have changed; people work remotely and have their own devices. They have an extra laptop that they bring with them to work or their personal phones. Some people end up using their personal phones for work stuff because it's just easier and quicker. Sometimes people bring home materials that they shouldn't bring home, or they use devices that may not be completely secure. What would you advise companies about these work protocols?

Cleve Adams: Let's face it, technology has made it possible to work from anywhere you have a smartphone and cellular signal, and using your personal device is often more convenient than a company issued one—especially if you just so happen to be out and about when a work issue comes up. Companies need to be diligent about security, but at the same time, they don't want to kill productivity.

For remote employees who work regularly from the same location—home, a shared workspace, and so on—you have **virtual private networks (VPNs)** to access company information resources. If they're just writing emails or looking at documents, sometimes this won't be necessary, but if they're talking back and forth with the corporate network, sharing sensitive corporate information, or sending collaboration documents out to different parts of the company, all that needs to be done with a VPN.

The good thing about VPNs these days is that they're easier to manage and more secure than ever. However, companies aren't using them on a regular basis. Ten years ago, everybody used VPNs to log into their networks, but today, that's not the case. Companies must create secure data networks that they can collaborate on.

Shira Rubinoff: Would you agree that there's a need to change the culture of companies when it comes to security?

Cleve Adams: Yes. A few years ago, we thought the biggest threat to enterprise was the personal cell phone; nearly as powerful as a desktop, but far more convenient to carry. Of course it was also far easier to lose or have stolen. Cloud services have eliminated a lot of that threat by keeping sensitive information off of the device and making it easy to wipe it remotely.

But now we're in the age of IoT, and literally everything from the building's light fixtures to the key fob in your pocket is now a potential attack vector, because they're generally poorly secured compared to the computers and servers on the network. We're living in a world where hackers can breach your network from a wireless thermostat, an IP camera, or 1,000 other devices no one gives much thought to. Corporate culture regarding cybersecurity needs to change from "don't worry about it, we're secure" to "security breaches can come from anywhere. Always be vigilant."

Shira Rubinoff: Cyber breaches are covered every day in the media. What would you say is the greatest threat to our enterprises? Is it insider risk? Is it ransomware? Is it more targeted attacks on cell phones and the like?

Cleve Adams: They're all risks. When I was at Websense, we focused not on keeping the bad guys out, but on keeping the bad guys from getting information out.

This meant trying to keep employees from going out and sharing documentation. That was content security. We found out that the insider threats were greater than the outsider threats, and I think that still applies today.

Companies are now getting smarter and more diligent about having their employees only log in from employee systems and asking them not to bring their cell phones in. This is especially true for ultra-secure organizations such as financial institutions and government entities. But breaches still happen. Outsiders coming inside your firm with their cell phones is a risk too.

As far as hacks and ransomware go, they are only going to continue; and it's only going to get worse. People are now hacking into cities and asking for $100,000 in ransom fees to get files decrypted. There are so many targets out there: large corporations, small corporations, cities, and individuals. We just need to be more diligent about how secure we are.

Shira Rubinoff: I'd like to bring up social media here. That's a massive area for leakage of information and also there's the risk of employees being socially engineered to trust somebody who will try to gain access to the business. For example, a high-ranking person at a competitor company reaches out to an intern at a large company wanting to connect. The intern is only thinking about their next job opportunity. The high-ranking person is not who they say they are and conversations between the two of them eventually lead to access being granted. What are your thoughts about social media when it comes to cybersecurity?

Cleve Adams: As far as I'm concerned, I don't trust any social network and its security. Every day, it seems that a site has been hacked and information has been stolen, or information has been sold by the social media platform itself to third parties.

If your company isn't on social media, you lose that additional marketing and press, but if you do sign up, hostile people will try to steal information. You just don't know what to do.

At Site 1001, we advertise jobs on LinkedIn, even though we shouldn't use social networks; they're unsecured platforms and your data can be sold at any time. I know I sound a little facetious but it's true.

If you look at Facebook, it's appalling that the company took data from corporations and individuals and sold that information to third parties. You just don't know what social networks are going to do. You only hope that their networks are secure and the data that you have put onto their networks is secure.

I'm on LinkedIn and Instagram because my company does a lot of marketing through those channels. They're deemed necessary now, so it's a very difficult situation.

Shira Rubinoff: What would you say about the situation I mentioned earlier where people end up trusting the wrong people and allow them access where access should not be granted?

Cleve Adams: So much of that is going on today. You have to be diligent and put together a security policy for social networking. You need to give only certain people within your company access to your social network profiles.

What employees do on their own time with social media is one thing, but you need to have security within your ranks about who has access to social media. A designated person needs to go out and make sure that communications are secure and that everything on social media is secure.

Shira Rubinoff: Let's talk about identity. Obviously, identity has evolved during your time in cybersecurity. Can you talk about that?

Cleve Adams: Identity and access go hand in hand these days. Access is always going to be a problem. Even back in the day when you didn't have the Internet and you had ID tags to get into secure locations, it was still an issue.

The difference today is that all these things are automated. Many companies are passing out **radio frequency identification (RFID)** tags, but if they get stolen and duplicated, then that's a security issue. There are tags now with chips in them and photographs. We're trying to do as many things as we can to keep identity and access secure, but criminals are criminals. People who want to get into your network, steal your identification, and steal your RFID tags are going to do so.

All you can do is be as diligent as you can be about the technology that you use for these things. Make sure it's up to date and secure. When you find out that badges have been stolen and identity has been accessed, then make sure that they are shut down immediately and erased.

Shira Rubinoff: In the past, we used our mother's maiden name or social security number for passwords. Now we're using thumbprints, but you could spoof those. Voice access is also a joke at this point, especially with AI moving so fast. That Facebook challenge, where people were posting a picture of themselves from 10 years ago and then a picture of themselves now, made me think about the data points being collected. What do you see as being a secure way of authenticating somebody?

Cleve Adams: There are different versions of authentication these days. There's the type where you use multiple passwords, which is two-step authentication, and then there's authentication where you have to select a bunch of pictures and check a box to make sure you're not a robot. Finally, there's authentication using information that you should know about yourself, such as security questions.

My company's authentication involves having strict guidelines on passwords. You need to change your password every 30 days. You need to come up with a password that has multiple capital letters, small letters, numbers, and symbols, and make sure it's not a word. Our authentication is not going to allow you to put "password123" in, for example. Believe me, I've seen "password123" used, and "1234567."

You could have two separate ways of authenticating employees. This could be thumbprints, retina scans, or two levels of passwords. However, the main thing that we need to recognize is that a simple password that can't be cracked is probably good enough, especially if you keep changing that password.

Right now, our passwords have to be 16 digits or 16 characters, which means you have to have a pretty good password. Obviously, the problem with that is that a lot of people will write it down somewhere. They keep it in their wallets, or even at the bottom of their desks.

I use a thumbprint on my phone to get in and also a passcode. So, if you stole my phone, you'd have to have my thumbprint and my passcode to get in, which is probably a deterrent. Use passwords, thumbprint identifications, and retina scans; use anything you can.

Shira Rubinoff: I was doing some consulting at a large financial institution, and walking through the offices I saw on a bunch of computers that had Post-its with passwords on. When I questioned them, the employees claimed that it didn't matter because they were all employees of the organization. I looked at them and asked, "Am I an employee of your organization? I now have the passwords to get into your system." Education within companies is important. How have your executive conversations changed over the last few years?

Cleve Adams: They've changed quite a bit. Security, passwords, and all the different types of authentication were never talked about in the past. Every once in a while, you would ask your employees when they last changed their password, but that was it.

Today, I think people are talking about security all the time and regularly changing their passwords. They see all these companies being hacked. Suddenly, data is out there. Hackers have names, phone numbers, addresses, credit cards, and so on. Even though people are being diligent about where they put their data, those companies are being hacked. It's very difficult to know what to do.

We, as a management team, have talked about security numerous times in our management meetings. How can we make the company more secure? How can we make sure our employees have the best passwords? How can we make sure that other companies will do business with us? Do they feel that we're adding another layer of trouble into their networks and their Internet connections?

You should have specialists. If you only have a CIO, that CIO should be trained on security methods. If you have a CISO, that person should be up to speed on all the latest and greatest security protocols and methods. I think that all companies need to take a look at their security and make critical decisions. It will come back to bite them if they don't.

Shira Rubinoff: Do you feel that it's imperative to have somebody who is fully educated around cybersecurity and can discuss risks with board members?

Cleve Adams: Yes, the board needs this information. Not in every board meeting, but on special calendared occasions there should be someone who is security-focused explaining the company's security protocols and how the board needs to follow them as well.

If the board members log in remotely to check their corporate emails, they need to be aware of security. There should be a session twice a year on that. I think that's all you need.

Shira Rubinoff: Have you ever been blown away by how at risk a company was?

Cleve Adams: Yes, there have been companies that thought they were very secure. For instance, I worked for a cybersecurity company a few years ago that was mainly focused on the government and how government organizations could be more secure with bring-your-own-devices.

The company found that people were bringing cell phones into Sensitive Compartmented Information Facilities (SCIFs). We all know that cell phones can be hacked and turned into listening devices or triggering devices. When you bring cell phones into locations that they shouldn't be in, that presents a problem.

One of the largest financial companies on Wall Street asked for help with security analysis. We were told that there were no unauthorized laptops, cell phones, iPads, or anything in the organization. So, we got our equipment out just to scan for devices. We told everybody in the company to turn all their equipment off. Then we turned our system on, which would detect any cellular activity.

Even if the cell phone was off and powered down, it would ping off a signal sometimes. Even though the company had powered them down, we found cell phones in one of the most secure organizations on the planet sitting in drawers, or in briefcases, or in coats that were hung in the closet in the lobby. Often, even though you think you're very secure, you're not. You need to double-check your security.

Websense went into companies that said they didn't need our products, because their content was secure and nobody did anything out of the ordinary on the Internet. We found that employees were doing things that they shouldn't be doing on the Internet, such as shopping, logging into their bank accounts, going to gambling sites, or going to pornography sites. It was pretty interesting to find out that one company thought that its employees were spending 100% of their time on productive activities. The fact that 68% of their employees were playing around was a big eye-opener.

Shira Rubinoff: Talking about cell phones, I don't think people even realize that some of their apps request permissions that are quite astounding. Would you agree?

Cleve Adams: Yes. If you think about it, you download an app and then you give it access to your photos, camera, and contacts. Most people don't pay any attention to that. They just respond, "Yes, yes, and yes."

The next thing they know, all of these apps have access to all their photographs and contact information. All the information that's on their phone and is supposed to be private is not. That's a problem.

When you walk into a company, an app can turn your phone into a camera, a listening device, a triggering device, and much worse. You need to be very careful about those types of apps and the permissions that you allow when you download them.

Shira Rubinoff: People could be doing everything right within an organization, but one small app on their phone could open them up to all sorts of problems, right?

Cleve Adams: Yes, it only takes one phone and one app for a hacker to have access to a corporate network and steal all the data.

Shira Rubinoff: Can an organization, or an individual, ever be truly cybersecure?

Cleve Adams: I used to think so, but I don't think so anymore. It seems that no matter what you do, the guys that want to break into your devices or your network are one step ahead of you.

We talked about this earlier, but hackers are hacking into very vulnerable networks of unexpected places. You might have a small town in Missouri, or Texas, that gets its town hall computers hacked into.

This could also happen to a hotel. Not only could hackers bring a hotel to its knees, but also, they could take data about its occupants. Hotels have all this personal information. It's not just corporations that are at risk. You need to stay one step ahead.

One thing that I read about the other night is that hackers hacked into a medical center, and all of its computer systems went down. The medical center had to pay a million dollars to get all its files back online. But in the 10 days that it didn't do this, it had to transfer all the patients out of the medical center and into a neighboring medical center. Everything had to move to pen and paper. Thousands and thousands of pieces of paper were written on and, in the end, it just wasn't worth the hassle. The medical center paid to get back online.

It's just amazing what's happening in this day and age with ransomware, and it's all automated. You can set up ransomware to attack a million people. If it gets into one or two computers, then you get your ransomware for the day. It's a big security issue that we need to stay on top of. Companies shouldn't think that because they're small and insignificant, they're safe.

Shira Rubinoff: Do you have any final thoughts about what you're excited about in cybersecurity?

Cleve Adams: I'm excited about the companies that are doing something about anomalies. For example, if your network does something every single day and, all of a sudden, it does something different, there's got to be something wrong with it. There's got to be a hack happening or somebody's opened a port they shouldn't have opened.

Products are getting better and security is getting better, but again, the bad guys are getting better as well. If you can adopt the latest technologies, I think you stand a much better chance.

Shira Rubinoff: Thank you, Cleve Adams.

Discussion

In the end, cybersecurity will have to continue to evolve and get more sophisticated to meet the new challenges of tomorrow. It's never going to get easier; old problems will be solved, but innovation will create new problems.

That's why it's your responsibility to remain abreast of the latest trends, and ensure your organization isn't falling behind the times. Your cyber defenses will be eclipsed by bad actors if you don't diligently follow what's happening in our world. You'll need to rise to the occasion when disaster strikes, and learn to prevent such events from happening in the future.

The risks of interconnectivity

IoT is changing the rules of cybersecurity. Both Barmak and Cleve highlight the fact that, in the recent past, there were fewer attack surfaces. Since the age of mainframes gave way to client-server computing and the internet, we saw a steady increase in attack surfaces. Today, IoT is only further accelerating that problem, as nearly any device that is connected is a possible attack surface that can be exploited and be used to facilitate a breach. Put simply, IoT is changing the rules for cybersecurity—we can't rely on older models as they will prove to be woefully inadequate in a world where interconnectivity is growing every day.

Increasing levels of interconnectivity will create interactions between technology that we have yet to see. For instance, Barmak sees autonomous cars being plugged into the environment around them, in effect helping each respective system function better. But with these technological interactions, you naturally increase the risk involved for nearly everyone using these technologies. We can hardly fathom the implications of a cyber breach on autonomous cars; one could cause many, many deaths in one fell swoop by triggering accidents on purpose. In the not-so-distant future, these types of threats may become mainstream, and challenge trust in technological progress.

Cleve points out how AI and machine learning are now taking hold in cybersecurity and how they're evolving in an environment where cyber intrusions and hacks are an inevitability. AI can help us stay ahead of these intrusions, and he believes that this predictive and adaptive technology will become standard in the near future.

Holistic cybersecurity

The magnitude of threats that will present themselves in an increasingly interconnected world require action by governments, the private sector and institutions of higher learning. Specifically, we have a dearth of talent that can adequately staff all of the organizations that require cybersecurity-focused personnel.

Moreover, the talent we have available isn't diverse in the slightest. This lack of diversity is problematic for cyber hygiene for reasons I've discussed in past chapters. In fact, Barmak doesn't see a sudden flood of cybersecurity talent on the horizon, and encourages all of us to automate our cybersecurity as much as possible. All options need to be on the table to be truly holistic in our endeavors.

Thinking more holistically means that staffing within an organization has to change to confront the new reality, that the movement to the cloud is decreasing the control you have over your digital assets. Additionally, security should be built into the fabric of IT assets. Being on the defensive always puts you at a strategic disadvantage because the hacker only has to get it right once—you have to get it right every time. This is where a holistic approach will help you get a better handle on your cyber defenses.

Cyber hygiene

Moreover, holistic cybersecurity means evolving past point products (products designed for a single specific security purpose) and viewing security in a more integrated way. I wholeheartedly agree with Barmak's assessment that we often make practicing proper cyber hygiene much more complex that it really has to be. We shouldn't have to tape together a bunch of point products and bedevil our organization with these piecemeal solutions.

We need to think big, and properly allocate our scarce resources toward tasks that truly matter and meaningfully contribute to bolstering our cybersecurity.

We often hear people screaming about the human disaster that will arise when automation and AI renders many jobs obsolete. Instead, as I've previously mentioned, we can use that "extra time" that we're saving from having obviated mundane tasks to improve our cyber hygiene. Given that there's not enough talent in the field of cybersecurity, perhaps we can draw from our talent pools and reskill or upskill employees to take over these positions that we desperately need people to occupy. As Barmak highlights, this is the "higher value-added" work that our human capital should be focused on, rather than wasting time on tasks that can be easily handled by a computer.

Cleve reveals that even the most secure organizations are at risk, especially if they believe that they've done everything to completely quash any cyber threat. Social media is a must in today's world, but as Cleve points out, social media networks are entirely unsecured, and they're apt to sell your data at any time. It's important to remember not to compromise your cyber hygiene with social media, as discussed in previous chapters.

People bring cell phones to places where they don't belong. They give permission to apps on their cell phones to outside applications, and then they use that very phone to perform work tasks. They log into websites on their work computers that can put them at risk. This is where the human factor comes in; never assume your organization's ranks are going to follow the rules. In fact, for proper cyber hygiene, you should probably instead imagine the worst-case scenario.

Security or efficiency?

We need a fundamental mindset reset on how we think about security and efficiency. We need to move away from the fallacy that one comes at the expense of the other. We also need to stop viewing different key people in the c-suite as having competing mandates as they pertain to cybersecurity.

We have to be aware, as Cleve mentions, that proper cyber hygiene is necessary to do business in this world. It isn't a checkbox, like the security culture of yesteryear; it is your entire organization's responsibility, and it ultimately determines your business' ability to thrive in today's world. If you're a victim of a public breach, your name is going to be mud for a while, and many people are going to pass up building new engagements with your business.

Therefore, we need to balance security and efficiency, and assure each other that the processes put into place fulfill both mandates without killing productivity. Cleve recommends leveraging secure data networks, so that organizations can remain secure even when their ranks are engaging in remote work.

Collaborative defenses

As Barmak mentioned, hackers are "smart and collaborative." If we are to be proactive as well as reactive, we have to follow the same playbook. The OTX is an example of how collaboration between organizations can be pivotal in the quest to remain proactive and reactive to fend off an ever-changing landscape of cyber threats.

Cleve insightfully discerns that people, and by extension organizations, are embarrassed to admit that their traumatic events caused a great deal of damage, and that this is a big stumbling block toward collaboration. This is where I believe it truly takes a village to have proper cyber hygiene. Collaboration, and shared commiseration, is a must.

Today, ransomware remains a major issue and there is no indication that it's going to go away. Instead, it's only going to continue unabated, and we need modern cybersecurity to address this growing problem. Hackers are targeting public and private organizations, causing massive damage, and even hamstringing the ability of these organizations to remain open for business. Perhaps cybersecurity will eventually evolve to solve this pressing problem, but another challenge will inevitably present itself.

Summary

Technological advancement is a constant factor that changes what it truly means to be cybersecure. Keeping up is a must in a world where both defenses and threats are fluid and rapidly evolving every moment of every day. When we think about cybersecurity, we need to consider the interplay of our organizations and the shifting landscape of the outside world as we integrate new technologies.

Fortunately, many of your industry peers face the same challenges you do, and that's why I can't stress collaboration enough. In an age where threats morph faster than many of our defenses, being in the know is critical to keep your organization and its data safe.

7

Staying Cybersecure in the IoT Revolution

Welcome to the age of IoT, where it's not just about connectivity; it's about amplifying the power of technology via digitization throughout the system. If you have "digital twins," replicas of data that are seamlessly transferred between two entities, you can leverage the data from IoT to make your processes more efficient, affordable, and nimble in fitting your changing needs.

Amid a promising future for IoT, we need to assess the way we view threats and cybersecurity in general. In a modern context, we need to move away from the mindset that we can avoid cyber threats entirely. In today's world with the advancement of IoT, threats are persistent and ever-changing, and you must approach your security from the vantage point that breaches have probably already happened under your watch.

IoT makes cybersecurity more complex, but it does so in an easily understandable way. As the number of connected but unmanaged devices increases, so does the risk. These devices, which may come into an organizational environment as legacy devices or newer devices, are sometimes not visible to the organization. This can create vulnerabilities that your organization isn't aware of at all. Therefore, you can mitigate these risks by knowing your data, a concept that I've returned to often throughout this book.

As both experts cover in their interviews, there is no one-size-fits-all cybersecurity solution for IoT, but protecting your organization begins with a stalwart framework of Zero Trust. With IoT, you must continually condition access, and leverage AI to constantly assess whether the device is behaving like it should at all times. The marriage of AI and Zero Trust with IoT will help maintain your cybersecurity in an environment where the proliferation of devices and entry points is quickly becoming the norm.

Barbara Humpton

Barbara Humpton has been the CEO of Siemens USA for a year and a half, with eight years of experience in the company. Inspired by expanding the horizon of what's humanly possible, Barbara guides her company's strategy and engagement with its U.S. market with a keen eye on the opportunities future technologies will create.

Shira Rubinoff: What's your background and what are you doing currently?

Barbara Humpton: Today, I serve as the CEO of Siemens USA. The U.S. is Siemens' largest market, making up about 25% of worldwide business. People aren't always familiar with Siemens, but we're a real leader in the infrastructure space, addressing the nation's needs across mobility, energy, and manufacturing.

I like to say we're into a new era of the "Internet of Really Big Things." This could be anything from power plants and transportation systems to significant healthcare capabilities. Electrification, automation, and digitalization are the core capabilities Siemens brings to the marketplace.

I've actually only been at Siemens for about eight years. When I started my career back in the '80s, I was with IBM. I was a math major and I joined IBM to learn how to do computer programming, which led to an absolutely fascinating career working on critical systems for national security.

I began with classified things, then I worked on the **Global Positioning System (GPS)**. After that, I worked on border security with Customs and Border Protection after 9/11, before ultimately working with the FBI on next-generation identification, which is the way that we identify criminals through biometrics.

The shape of my career was driven by the challenge of applying bleeding-edge technologies to big problems. The first half of my career was focused on national security, whereas at Siemens our work extends around the globe. We're able to take best practices, bring them into local markets, and help our customers to take advantage of these truly industry-leading concepts.

Shira Rubinoff: Can you describe how Siemens is using IoT connectivity?

Barbara Humpton: When I was first learning about Siemens' experience in this regard, one of the great stories that the team came back with was that in 1977, we first connected a gas turbine to headquarters. It was located at a customer's premises, but it connected back to the mother ship for information flow.

This was well before we had the Internet as we now know it; it was in the early days of computing. Siemens has long understood the power of being able to transcend time and space with information that can help with the real operations of physical assets. We've gone from working in the power industry and finding ways to make power generation technology more capable; and now we're bringing connectivity into manufacturing through what we call the digital enterprise.

For the infrastructure around us, what we're trying to create, in essence, are digital twins. These digital twins produce a great deal of data that can be used to make the infrastructure more effective, less expensive, and more responsive to the environment.

Shira Rubinoff: What would you say are the main ways that we can keep our industries or our companies secure when dealing with the digitalization of IoT?

Barbara Humpton: There's a well-known phrase about this: "There are two kinds of people in the world: the people who know they've been hacked and the people who've been hacked and just don't know it."

As soon as computers came along, and as soon as communications began to connect things, the threat existed. I think the most important thing for everyone to be aware of today is that the cyber threat is real and it's already inside companies.

You should no longer be asking, "How can I keep things out?" You have to operate with the knowledge that you probably have already been infiltrated. Now you should be asking, "How do I protect my operations and maintain continuity for my customers?"

You can't defeat an enemy that you can't see. What's necessary is to be able to use data analytics. It's important for people who operate digital systems to have operating environments that make use of the best capabilities available to us today.

Three broad questions must be asked: 1) How do you detect that you're experiencing an attack? 2) What tools can you give to operators to help them to respond and repair their environments? 3) How do you figure out what has been exploited and what harm may have been done to your enterprise?

I think it's important now, more than ever, to realize that we're living in a world where this is part of normal business operations. I'm trying to use my voice to help people to understand persistent threats. Rather than attempting to avoid cyber attacks, companies need to embrace the concept that they are already upon them, and now there are certain things that they need to do as normal practice.

Shira Rubinoff: When it comes to cybersecurity in general, the big topic is knowing where your data is and who has access to it. What advice can you give to organizations and companies around this?

Barbara Humpton: I think the future is going to be all about trust. A digital economy is going to be built up over time and its foundation will be trust as people seek to gain more control over their information. Many people want to know where their data is physically stored, but I actually think they're undermining their own goals in the process.

I'll give an example: a utility customer wanted its data to stay on-site, which meant providing security of its own and attending to all of the ongoing and evolving threats. There aren't enough resources in this world, or enough cyber talent, for us to create what I call "separate castles and moats" for every business.

What I've been trying to share with companies is that they need to embrace the concept of security in the cloud. I understand that companies want to know where their data is physically and that it's safe, but it is in fact safer in the cloud because it's in the hands of professionals who have the resources to provide leading security protection. They possess the ability to evolve in response to a threat. There is greater security in what's provided now in cloud computing.

There's one thing to keep in mind, though, which is that companies moving to the cloud do need to choose wisely. As in anything else, not all offerings are created equal. So as part of our shift to the cloud, companies just need to make sure they're getting the right security levels and partnerships to support their desired connectivity.

Shira Rubinoff: When it comes to companies utilizing IoT, what would you say are your top three pieces of advice for maintaining cybersecurity?

Barbara Humpton: Firstly, on the technical front, it's vitally important to now embrace the concept of the cloud, as I just mentioned, and take advantage of the wisdom of the crowd in managing assets.

My second piece of advice is that companies should understand what their precious core is, but they should also successfully partner with cyber professionals, either in a cloud-type environment or in some other framework. They should engage with experts in the field of cybersecurity.

Thirdly, this isn't a technical problem in most cases; this is a people problem. The best analogy for where we are in cybersecurity and IoT is what we've done in the area of physical security, such as environmental health and safety and **Occupational Safety and Health Administration** (**OSHA**).

In the past, it was not uncommon for people to be injured in the day-to-day course of their jobs. Companies sent people into harm's way when, for example, climbing electricity poles. Since then, we've created health and safety protocols, training regimens, and cultural programs within companies that have helped people to understand that achieving zero accidents is possible. We've learned that following the right practices and taking care of each other can reduce the threats to life and limb.

We can take this same concept and apply it to cybersecurity. I think there's a lot we can learn. I'm encouraging companies to drive their cultural change in that manner.

I think we've enjoyed, over the last decade, treating cyber as if it's this magical dark arts area. In fact, there are some really practical and no-nonsense practices that can improve our overall cyber position. By ingraining these principles into company cultures and making them accessible to all employees, we can help people to understand what their responsibility is when it comes to cyber.

Shira Rubinoff: Where else do you think that we need to tighten up around cybersecurity?

Barbara Humpton: There are no national boundaries in cyberspace. I know that nations have controlled access to the Internet through communications, but in reality, there aren't national borders for that.

Yet, all around the globe, we have local cyber regulation. A patchwork of rules and regulations has grown naturally because every single government around the world wants to protect its citizens. There is good cause for wanting to do so, but my sense is that what needs to happen now is an industry coalition. Leaders across government and the private sector need to work with one another to agree on how to build our applications.

There's a real need in cybersecurity for the private sector to take a leadership role in advancing the right standards and best practices. I don't think we should be driven and led by government regulation. That should be the default only if we're unable to solve problems as businesses. The makers of technologies need to take the lead and put forward their assertions about what it will take to be trustworthy in the new future economy.

Shira Rubinoff: Do you have any stories that illustrate best practices or horror stories that you've seen around cyber and IoT?

Barbara Humpton: I can tell you a story about Siemens' technology from about five years ago. With connected devices, the idea is that you can have a USB port and it enables you to link up all kinds of different technologies.

Everybody thought it was cool to be interconnected and we had a new product that came out from one of our businesses. It was a control system mounted on a wall that came with a USB port in it. This meant that a building owner, walking around a facility, could have stuck a USB connector into this port. They would suddenly have had access to that control system. That was shockingly unacceptable.

What solved the problem was super glue. People all around the country were going around their buildings with little tubes of super glue and closing up USB ports. We laugh about it now, but that type of thing is a serious problem. We're aware of things like the Target hack, so we know that the threat is real.

Shira Rubinoff: With the IoT revolution, we have all these interconnected devices and wearables. We also have third-party organizations and software grabbing the data from them and utilizing it in different ways that customers might not know about. How do you feel about the IoT revolution when it comes to these types of issues?

Barbara Humpton: We're about to hit this turning point in the debate of privacy versus convenience. With everything that's happened in the last couple of years around social media breaches, there's been a public outcry. Despite that, I don't think these news stories have actually changed our behaviors very much.

As a society, we value the convenience and the efficiency of being able to have our data at our fingertips, even if that means that there's a risk that our data may leak out.

We're trying to get to a stage where the individual has control of their data. There's now the idea that being able to control one's own data is a fundamental right. I may choose to share more than the person next to me, because the person next to me may decide to give up some convenience in favor of greater privacy.

That's a noble goal, but the only thing I question is whether it's truly realistic. We're back to that fundamental discussion; if something is digital, it's hackable. End of story. We're going to need some creative approaches as we move forward to protect our golden nuggets of information.

Shira Rubinoff: What would you say to people who are afraid of the impact that technology will have?

Barbara Humpton: Throughout my career, I've embraced technology, but I do recognize that there's real fear about the societal impact of many emerging technologies, whether that's a robot replacing a worker or an autonomous vehicle getting taken over by a hacker.

Just this week, I was having a discussion, and almost an argument, with some people about whether technology is to be feared. Is there a moment when technology is going to supersede us? I'm a firm believer that it won't.

Technology has always helped us to expand what's humanly possible and elevate the role of the human. These new tools just enhance the way that we live our lives, what we're able to create, and even what we can imagine.

Even on the subject of cybersecurity, I find it to be fascinating rather than terrifying. Cybersecurity is challenging rather than paralyzing. You have to open yourself up to and face these challenges; you can't hide from them. And we do need to address the real challenges that are present. Technology is changing some jobs, but we also can tailor our workforce development strategies in a way that leave no one behind. Yes, technology is creating some security challenges, yet it's also opening up opportunities to make systems and infrastructure safer too. The future is ours to shape.

Shira Rubinoff: When we talk about cybersecurity, we have to talk about leadership. Your background certainly lends itself to that. What can you share about what type of leadership is needed to address cybersecurity challenges?

Barbara Humpton: We need to invest in people. There was an article that I recently read that said cybersecurity professionals are the online world's firefighters. We need heroes who are willing to go to the front line.

We're seeing the explosion of digital. In the U.S., we have half a million open jobs for computer programmers. For cyber, most organizations are still catching up, so we're seeing cyber positions growing faster than IT positions.

Within two years, we're expecting to see about 3.5 million unfilled cyber jobs worldwide. The numbers are staggering. We have to think about this as businesses. We need to work alongside the public sector, especially the education system, to educate the people who may have a talent for this kind of work. What we've been doing is reaching out to universities, but also then reaching out into the community college system. As we move into an age of lifelong learning, because technology is transitioning so quickly, people will need to be committed to continuing their education throughout their careers.

Shira Rubinoff: What would you say to anyone thinking about entering the cybersecurity field? In the past, people would envision cybersecurity professionals to be sitting in their hoodies in basements.

Barbara Humpton: I would encourage people to enter this space because it's central to every business strategy today and to see the whole spectrum of opportunities. There's a lot of focus on the consumer side, and many still see cybersecurity as something that exists separate from day-to-day business or the larger goals of an organization. But there's far more work now being done in product design in partnership with engineers and project managers working with industry, cities, and infrastructure. This work is helping to shape the actual products and services that are being brought to market.

You have the opportunity to work with business leaders, along with those working on the commercial side of the business and the business proposition itself. There are roles in the back office, as well as in the front office dealing with customers. This position touches every aspect of the enterprise. Particularly for a young person entering business today, the opportunity to start somewhere in an organization and end up nearly anywhere is what cyber offers.

Shira Rubinoff: Do you have any last thoughts to share around IoT?

Barbara Humpton: IoT is in its infancy. What we don't know yet is where this is going to lead us. I can't wait to see the creativity of the business and technical minds around us, as they start to take advantage of what the technical tools allow us to do.

Now that we can connect things that have never been connected before, think about all the new ways we can arrange our lives and arrange the work that we do. The infrastructure that we've built around us can be so much more responsive to our wants and needs with IoT.

Think back to 2007. The iPhone came out and an explosion followed. Look at the convergence of technologies needed to make that possible. All of us who were dealing with old forms of communication, entertainment, and access to media could never have even dreamed we'd be where we are 10 years later. I feel that way now about IoT.

Shira Rubinoff: Thank you, Barbara Humpton.

Ann Johnson

Ann Johnson is the Corporate Vice President of the Cybersecurity Solutions Group at Microsoft, overseeing the go-to-market strategies of cybersecurity for the business. Having worked previously as a CEO and COO, Ann has a broad outlook on cybersecurity and a mandate to align long- and short-term solutions for one of the largest tech companies on the planet.

Shira Rubinoff: Could you explain a little bit about your background and your role at Microsoft?

Ann Johnson: I've spent the last three years at Microsoft. I was recruited to focus on building out our security business, so I'm responsible for our security and compliance business globally.

That includes our global incident response practice, some of our security offerings for customers, evangelism, advocacy, direct sales, and anything that's related to actually bringing security and compliance solutions to our customers; really driving modernization, and driving our customers toward cloud security.

Prior to Microsoft, I was in the technology sector for a total of 30 years and I've been in security since 2000. I spent almost 14 years at RSA Security. Prior to my security career, I was focused largely on infrastructure, network, and storage. I have a pretty strong infrastructure background, which I can tell you is very helpful when you want to have a security career.

Shira Rubinoff: You wrote a blog titled *The AI cybersecurity impact for IoT*. What was the inspiration for this post?

Ann Johnson: The inspiration was as follows: I spent a lot of time engaging with customers and I had been traveling to many different parts of the globe. Customers I met with were trying to build solutions, bring them to market, and really leverage automated technologies.

There is a commonality of concern, regardless of the industry or the geography of a customer: the tremendous amount of unmanaged IoT devices coming into environments, whether those are legacy devices or newer devices. Customers really don't have the ability to manage these devices in the way they would have managed, say, a PC coming into the environment, or a mini computer, or a mainframe. There's concern that there isn't visibility around these devices and they can't be managed.

For example, there was one particular customer in Australia that wanted to have fully automated mining operations in remote parts of the country so the company didn't have to actually put people on the ground. However, each vehicle had hundreds of sensors in it, and hundreds of IoT centers, so the company was very concerned about security in the operations, both physical and logical.

I was talking to banks about their ATM networks, and also talking to healthcare organizations about what they were doing with patient care. Suddenly, all of this came together in my mind. As an industry, we don't have great solutions for customers yet and I would group those solutions into two buckets: solutions for legacy IoT centers that were never built to be managed from a secure standpoint—in a lot of cases you can't even change the passwords—and also the newer solutions that are coming to market, along with questions about how we can actually build in security for things like Azure Sphere. How do we build in security from the ground up? This led me to write a blog because it seemed to be both a top-of-mind concern for customers, and something that as an industry, we really do need to try to solve.

Shira Rubinoff: Certainly, there's a lot of talk and your main customers are concerned, but in general, do you think that cybersecurity is a big concern right now when dealing with IoT?

Ann Johnson: Cybersecurity is one of the greatest concerns when dealing with IoT. Customers are saying, "Look, we're going to have this influx of devices. We already have this influx of devices and we're really concerned about the behavior of those devices as they come into the environment, regardless of how they're coming in."

I want to emphasize that the interesting thing to me is that this isn't just a concern from a security standpoint, it's also a concern for business leaders because they don't want to jeopardize their brand, or jeopardize their business operations with these types of devices as they build solutions for the future.

Shira Rubinoff: How do organizations secure their environments from a potential attack, unknown to them, from an IoT device? There are many different areas that the attack could come from. What should they do?

Ann Johnson: I'm always a big believer in "defense in depth." I don't ever think there's just one solution. If you think about companies that are doing vulnerability management-type solutions, those solutions need to be able to actually understand the firmware, or the hardware, or the software on those IoT devices, to the extent that they can. That's the first step.

The second point is that at Microsoft, we're really promoting, as well as a lot of companies in the industry, the concept of Zero Trust networks. With a Zero Trust network, you're not trusting anything that's coming into your environment. If you take the stance to not trust anything, you're going to inspect everything.

When you think about security, think about identity in the context of a Zero Trust network. Identity is no longer just the human: it's the device, the data, the application, and its location. So, we want to make sure that we not only look at the device when it comes onto the network, but we actually have continual conditional access with that device.

Even if we can't get all of the forensic evidence we want from the device when it first comes onto the network, we should be able to maintain a model of behavior and say, "Okay, this device is actually not behaving in a manner that we would expect a device in this class to behave in, so we're going to do something to stop it from interacting on our network until we can further verify it."

It's about looking for known vulnerabilities, the authentication of the device, the application, the data, the user, and where they're physically located. Then you look at all the behavioral aspects and ask, "Is this device behaving in an expected manner, or are there anomalies?"

When I wrote my blog, I talked about how, although I don't believe in silver bullets, if I think about the practical applications of **artificial intelligence (AI)**, it's one of the things that can really help with IoT. An example I gave in the blog was if you're a cardiac care unit in a hospital and you have devices that have been doing cardiac care for however many years. Suddenly, either you change manufacturers, or the manufacturer changes the device. You should still be able to identify the device as a certain class of device, without ever having seen the new device previously.

You can use machine learning for behavioral modeling to say, "Here's how it is expected to behave. If the device doesn't behave in that manner and is anomalous, we can actually do something to block it, or to further quarantine it." That's something that I'm really passionate about.

I don't think there is a one-size-fits-all solution for IoT. I think that IoT is going to be driven by how you can actually protect your environment, and that starts with having a really good framework for Zero Trust. It starts with having defense in depth and it starts with using technologies such as continual conditional access to maintain visibility on the state of the device.

Shira Rubinoff: Can you give any real-world examples of any situations where you saw IoT being utilized, but the security was just not there? Have breaches occurred that you could share?

Ann Johnson: Without naming customers specifically, there have been many attacks launched on ATM environments. The interesting thing about ATM environments is that they're typically running a full OS, but they are still accessing the network in a manner that looks like an IoT device.

There have been attacks that have been launched on healthcare organizations specific to the types of devices we're discussing, and the impact of that hasn't been so much data leakage, but rather interrupted operations. The ability to interrupt operations and cause the financial deprecation of operations is something that is, I think, significant for organizations from a brand standpoint, but also from a revenue standpoint.

Shira Rubinoff: Do you think vulnerability management will continue to be a critical aspect of IoT security, and what are some other key considerations?

Ann Johnson: Vulnerability management and legacy vulnerability management solutions are really good from an actual full-OS standpoint. If you think about some of the newer players, such as CyberX; or Dragos; or those type of companies that are coming in and doing specific vulnerability management, but also have a lot more breadth with regard to IoT devices, I don't think there will be a time in our industry when vulnerability management capabilities aren't going to be required.

Because software and security are constantly evolving, we're never going to get to a time where we're perfectly coding software. Therefore, software will likely always go out with bugs in it. The goal is to reduce those bugs as much as we can. If you think about IoT devices, they're always going to have some type of vulnerability in them for the most part. I'm not trying to be a fatalist; it's just one of those natural things about building software.

In order to actually protect your environment, you need something that's going to detect those vulnerabilities, both on your full-OS systems and on your iOS IoT devices. There will always be a need for it, but I do think the technology needs to evolve.

Shira Rubinoff: Do you believe there'll be a standard put in place for IoT devices that they will all have to adhere to in order to be completely secure?

Ann Johnson: I think there's a need for a standard, but the question would be whether or not this is realistic. As an industry, we're great at standards. I do think, unfortunately, what's going to happen is that it's going to take a very large attack for people to a) get standards, and b) do the proper regulation, and the proper regulation without doing too much regulation. I just think that it's going to take an event because that's how many of these things evolve.

Shira Rubinoff: As of today, have there been any large attacks that you want to discuss?

Ann Johnson: The biggest one would be Mirai, a couple of years ago, where there was a large **distributed denial-of-service (DDoS)** attack in the U.S. The challenge with that attack was that it wasn't specific to IoT. It was specific to DDoS technologies that could have been deployed against any type of infrastructure.

It raises eyebrows when people say, "Oh wow, that's fully IoT." I do think the attacks have been fairly isolated and they haven't been publicized much, which is surprising to me, but that will come; you know it will.

Shira Rubinoff: Where do you see AI having the biggest impact for IoT devices? I know we discussed the blog post, but do you have anything specific around AI and IoT with cyber intertwined?

Ann Johnson: I think the biggest impact is with those devices that were previously not recognized; you've never seen those types of devices before, or even that class of device.

You should be able to be use predictive AI to understand how the device should be behaving, and that will be a change for the industry because typically, when we build whitelists and blacklists, and we build behavioral models, we assume a 90- to 120-day baseline of information about how something is going to behave, whether it's a user or a device. We're not going to have that luxury with the volume of IoT devices coming in and the speed at which this is happening.

As I mentioned earlier, the ability for AI to say, "This device isn't behaving in an expected manner based on other devices that I am seeing and I'm aware of," and actually model what that behavior should look like, will have the biggest impact because that will then give the customer confidence that they can actually bring previously unknown or unseen devices into their environment and they don't have to wait for that long modeling period. Think about it like how AI is being used today to detect previously unknown versions of malware, which is a very similar technology.

Shira Rubinoff: Do you see a difference in terms of IoT devices from other countries? Would you be worried about implementing different devices without specific protocols?

Ann Johnson: Without making a geopolitical statement, yes. I will tell you that there are certain regions of the world that we always consider riskier than other regions of the world. Regardless of whether it's a device, or a person, or a computer from those regions of the world, we would have an increased level of concern.

Shira Rubinoff: Coming down to it, what would you say are your top pieces of security advice for organizations when it comes to IoT and IoT security?

Ann Johnson: Don't look for that silver bullet solution for just IoT. You have your security policies; you know what your risk management profile and risk appetite are. So, my primary piece of advice is: don't change your security policies just because of IoT.

Yes, IoT probably has increased your risk, but you still know what the risk appetite of your organization is and you should be adhering to your standard security policies. No solution is going to solve everything, as much as we would like it to.

One interesting development is that Microsoft has partnered to build a fully baked Linux OS on top of a hardened chip for new IoT implementations. There are other instantiations of this in the industry; it's not just Microsoft, though I think we've done a very good job of getting the Azure Sphere solution to market.

My other piece of advice is that if you're going to build new IoT devices, look for those secure solutions, so you're actually building those devices on top of a fully hardened OS. That way, the ability to actually breach those devices is much less. As you're building new technologies for IoT, make sure you're using a hardened environment.

Shira Rubinoff: When it comes down to investments around these types of solutions, where do you see the security community making investments to secure IoT devices today? How will AI enhance those efforts over time?

Ann Johnson: Dark Reading put out a study in July of last year about where security practitioners are spending their money, and you'd be surprised: they're still spending it in the same places, which is endpoint networks, and so on.

What I did not see was a classification specifically for IoT. I suspect that it's combined under that endpoint network security spend. I know organizations are spending money on IoT security. I don't think they're doing this discretely and it's probably now part of their endpoint budgets.

Organizations are starting to spend more money on AI-type technologies. When I say AI-type technologies, it's more about humans, by the way. AI is very human-dependent from a building and modeling standpoint, at least in its early stages. As AI gets more mature in an organization, it will need less human capital, but what I see is human spend on AI and IoT being still in the network and endpoint security buckets.

Shira Rubinoff: What criteria should be considered when deciding whether a device is a candidate for IoT?

Ann Johnson: I think that if you have a device that doesn't need human intervention, it's probably a good candidate for IoT, as opposed to a computer, which requires you to do something with it every day.

My refrigerator at home could phone when it needs a repair and that wouldn't require any interaction on my part. When we take this idea out to commercial applications, offshore oil reading is a conversation we've been having. Companies want that to be fully automated, just from a physical security standpoint. Mining is another application. A computer will run from a remote location and make sure that the devices (they are physical devices) are operating those drills or operating properly. So, those are great applications for IoT.

Think about people who are doing any type of manufacturing, whether it's pharmaceutical, or hard materials-type manufacturing. Any of those activities are great applications for IoT devices because people are trying to do more modernization and more automation, and in doing that, they're going to work more IoT into their environments.

Shira Rubinoff: Many people say they're worried about things moving more toward IoT because jobs will disappear. What are your thoughts about jobs actually being created rather than depleted utilizing IoT technology?

Ann Johnson: I absolutely don't agree with the fear of jobs reducing. We find that AI and machine learning, and all of those models, work better with humans involved. AI just makes humans work better and work smarter.

So, we will create different classes of jobs, but there still will need to be operators; they're just not necessarily going to be operators on a line physically putting something together. They may be operators that are operating the machines that are putting things together. I think that IoT technology will create different types of jobs, but it's still going to create them.

Shira Rubinoff: Thank you, Ann Johnson, for taking the time to share your thoughts.

Discussion

The good news is that IoT doesn't mean that security policy needs to be entirely rewritten, as a lot of the same rules that I've covered in depth apply. Training, global awareness, security, and Zero Trust are extremely relevant in this chapter, as is procuring devices that are built from the ground up with security considerations in mind. Understanding people, processes, and technology is still the bedrock of effective cybersecurity within your organization, and IoT is a just another item on the growing list of responsibilities for cybersecurity professionals.

Cultural change

Barbara offers excellent advice for organizations when she points out that cultural change must be driven from within. She puts emphasis on practical and no-nonsense policies that are imperative to maintaining your cyber hygiene in the age of IoT. Moreover, she touches on a theme that I repeat throughout this book regarding the shared nature of responsibility in cybersecurity. It's no longer a niche area confined to certain members whose work duties exclusively involve keeping your digital assets safe. Instead, cybersecurity and cyber hygiene is a shared responsibility that requires 100 percent participation and awareness among your organizational ranks, from top to bottom. As your entry points to your system proliferate with IoT, this principle is more important than ever. As Barbara poignantly reminds us, we have to really think about our workforce development strategies so that nobody is left behind.

It's important to revisit human factors when we're thinking about cybersecurity, especially with IoT. If it's a hassle to keep our data secure, most people are going to cut corners and expose themselves and their respective organizations to a great deal of risk. Despite all of the high-profile data breaches, Barbara points out that people haven't really changed their behavior. We put our heads in the sand when we're presented with new information that tells us our habits might be far too risky in today's climate.

Ann drives home that because of human nature, it often takes a crisis before we establish benchmarks and protocols for keeping our organizations secure, and IoT devices are no exception to this phenomenon.

Attacks specifically involving IoT haven't been heavily publicized, but they do happen and once it comes, you can bet there are going to be giant leaps in the promulgation of standards and regulations by industry groups and governments.

The IoT training gap

Training in cybersecurity specifically for IoT has yet to mature in the field. As Ann mentioned, we don't even know how much security practitioners are spending on security for IoT because it's not a demarcated category. We know organizations are taking IoT into account in their training, but we can't enumerate just how much a budget is going toward managing their risks in an environment of ever-increasing interconnectivity.

Lastly, training is challenging as there is an acute shortage of cybersecurity professionals. Barbara talked about the dire statistics that the industry faces, as there will be more than 3.5 million unfilled jobs in the next two years. In this climate, we must be forward-thinking in our training plans and embed continuing education for all employees in our training protocol. Lifelong learning for every single person in your organization is no longer an option—it's a must in an age where obsolescence is just around the corner.

Global IoT collaboration

The global awareness component of maintaining your cybersecurity posture in the IoT revolution inevitably involves gleaning the lessons learned from your industry peers. The good news is you don't have to reinvent the wheel: just like there were enormous leaps in workplace safety protocols over the years, there are many, many resources for cybersecurity professionals in a changing environment.

While lessons learned are a good start, I couldn't agree with Barbara more that we need an industry coalition to promulgate best practices in cybersecurity. While governments are beginning to roll out their piecemeal approaches to cyber regulations, this alone will not be enough to be cybersecure. As Barbara reminds us, there are no national boundaries in cyberspace, so we're going to have to think globally when tackling our biggest security challenges.

Taking a leadership role to roll out best practices will require cooperation. Fortunately, as an industry we have begun to understand the importance of information sharing within our ecosystem. Moving forward, we need to band together as industry peers to create the right standards, applying intel and lessons learned from all of our organizations. Getting ahead of the curve will mean that we won't need government regulation to address the problem, which can get messy quickly, and governments often overreact with regulatory policy and stifle innovation and profitability.

Thinking about the effect of IoT globally, we should embrace it as the next chapter in essential technological progress. Ann sees IoT creating different types of jobs and that, much like AI and machine learning, it will make humans smarter and more efficient. If leveraged properly, it will also make your cyber hygiene better.

People need to understand IoT and how it can magnify and optimize the work that they do. It's not coming for their job; it's instead going to make their lives better. Interconnectivity is a boon for productivity, and globally this will be a giant leap forward for our workflow and our day-to-day operations.

IoT-specific risks

As Barbara says, if something is digital it is hackable, which is certainly relevant to IoT-type breaches. There is always going to be a tenuous balance between privacy and convenience. Ann talks about how we live in a culture of convenience and connectivity, and that influences the way we view technological solutions. Smart devices are becoming the norm in the private sector and in our everyday consumer lives. These devices are making our lives easier to manage and facilitating productivity and connectivity for a world that was previously fragmented. These advancements in connectivity provide many positive attributes while in turn also creating a litany of cybersecurity risks.

Ann stresses a common risk concern that is highlighted when it comes to IoT: the proliferation of unmanaged devices. These devices, which may come into an organizational environment as legacy devices or newer devices, are sometimes not visible to the organization.

There is a lack of direct control with IoT devices, and as we saw in the example of her Australian customer, some organizations simply don't know their data.

As we've covered, knowing your data—where it sits, who has access to it, and what security is implemented around it—is needed to keep the data secure. Following these steps under knowing your data is the linchpin of cybersecurity, and it's very relevant to the security problems that present themselves in IoT. AI is going to help us understand how a device is behaving and can help you skip over the modeling period, saving a great deal of time and resources.

Vulnerability management

I'd like to echo Ann's view on the critical role of vulnerability management in IoT security: the need for these capabilities is never going to go away. Software is created by humans and accordingly will always be flawed one way or another. IoT devices will always have some sort of vulnerability that needs to be addressed, and that's an important part of keeping your organization safe.

As I've mentioned, infiltration into your systems is a reality that we all have to live with on a daily basis. It's not a matter of if you'll suffer a breach, it's a matter of when, and how you recover from that incident and implement lessons learned. This is where data analytics plays a key role in managing cyber threats, as Barbara covers, detecting breaches, deploying a coordinated response, and assessing what damage has been done.

Barbara calls cybersecurity professionals the "online world's firefighters," and I think that's a great way to view our work and the nature of our role. Security as it pertains to IoT means that we're always going to be on the front line putting out fires. We're going to have to continuously monitor device behavior with 100 percent adherence to a Zero Trust model.

Zero Trust and IoT

I can't stress enough that Zero Trust is at the heart of protecting your organization in a landscape where IoT has become the expected norm. As you get an influx of devices, your bulwark against cyber risks is having a Zero Trust network. If you don't practice Zero Trust, you could be, as Ann warns, jeopardizing your reputation of even your entire business operations.

Things that we once took as a static component are changing as technology advances and redefines even the most basic concepts in cybersecurity. Ann stops and reminds us that even the concept of identity is changing in today's technological ecosystem, as it has ceased to be only human. Devices, data, and applications also have identities, and this is where Zero Trust and continuous conditional access are key to keeping your organization secure.

In sum, Zero Trust means Zero Trust—no exceptions. In an environment where the proliferation of devices means that entry points are growing faster than anyone can account for, Zero Trust is the only way. We must position ourselves for the cyberwars that are currently occurring, along with the ones that are inevitably not too far off in the future.

Summary

IoT is the next chapter of digital interconnectedness and can't be avoided by consumers and businesses alike. Still, IoT is accompanied by risks due to the increased surface area from which your data can be lifted more easily. Barbara and Ann gave great advice on how a proactive security posture that actively seeks breaches before they occur is the only way to navigate a world in which IoT is the norm.

Before I move on to our next chapter, I'll leave you with my favorite quote from Barbara: "There are two kinds of people in the world: the people who know they've been hacked and the people who've been hacked and just don't know it." You need to be in the know about the hacking that might be occurring while you're sitting here reading this book.

8

Cyberwars – Bringing Military Lessons to Modern Information Security

We often think of war as hostilities between nation states or organized rogue entities, intended to pursue strategic interests and secure victory. Warfare itself has not changed, but the emergence of the digital world has added an extra layer to the nature of war. While nation states and subnational entities are still tussling for power and control in various spheres of interest, the digital world provides another medium for war, where victories, big and small, can be secured without a single bullet.

Unlike traditional warfare, in cyberwarfare players aren't limited to governments, terrorist groups, or other entities that have traditionally duked it out on the battlefield. The modern battlefield has been digitized, meaning that anyone, anywhere, can become a target of a concerted effort to compromise your cyber defenses. Threats can come from anywhere at any time, and often the bad actors are far from identifiable.

I recognize that there is a great deal of disagreement as to what exactly constitutes a cyberwar. While we can't all agree on an exact definition, we do know that every single person and organization on the planet who uses a computer is at risk of data theft.

I believe that cyberwars are sustained hostilities engendered by a wide variety of bad actors, who can be rogue or affiliated with nation states, with the intended purpose of stealing data from their target or targets. Both targets and bad actors can be governments, organizations, or even individuals. In many cases, much like classic warfare, cyberwars serve a militaristic purpose to weaken an enemy, even if the target is a non-governmental entity.

Given the similarities between cyberwarfare and classic warfare, it's only logical that military strategy can offer excellent insight into keeping your data safe. Applying military discipline to information governance means viewing data security through a multifaceted lens, that considers a wide array of avenues of attack as well as human factors that frequently compromise our established cyber defenses.

Brigadier General Gregory Touhill has witnessed firsthand the rise of computers and how they quickly become weaponized for nefarious purposes. Through his career journey and insight, we'll explore, amid the raging cyberwars, what you can do to keep your data out of the hands of harmful actors. Throughout our interview, you'll discover the core concepts of military-level digital hygiene and how they're relevant to the corporate world.

Brigadier General Gregory Touhill

Gregory Touhill was appointed by President Barack Obama as the U.S. government's first Chief Information Security Officer (CISO). His other civilian government service includes duties as the Deputy Assistant Secretary for Cybersecurity and Communications in the U.S. Department of Homeland Security and as Director of the National Cybersecurity and Communications Integration Center where he led national programs to protect the United States and its critical infrastructure.

Greg currently serves as President of Cyxtera Federal Group, and as a member of several corporate and non-profit boards of directors. He is an adjunct professor of cybersecurity at both Carnegie Mellon and Georgetown Universities.

Shira Rubinoff: Please could you explain a little bit about your background and your career history?

Brigadier General Gregory Touhill: I had a thirty-year career in the U.S. Air Force. Computers and electronics were my starting point, but I also grew up in the era when we realized, to paraphrase James T. Kirk's son, that computers could be perverted into dreadful weapons.

During my career in the Air Force, we not only worked on how to defend using computers, but we also explored how we could use computers as part of a combined-arms approach to the military—using computers and the technologies out there to better protect our country and achieve our goals. Information technology has permeated every part of our society.

At the time of my retirement from active duty I was one of the Defense Department's Senior Cybersecurity Officers, and at one point led the Air Force's cyberspace training for all of the airmen in the Air Force. After that I served as the Deputy Assistant Secretary of Homeland Security in the Office of Cybersecurity and Communications.

After leading incident response at the United States Office of Personnel Management, I served as the U.S. Government's first Chief Information Security Officer.

I was drawn to come to Cyxtera when it was founded in May of 2017. Cyxtera's mission is the same as mine—to better protect national prosperity and national security. Frankly, I don't think you can have one without the other.

Cyxtera provides some impressive transformational capabilities, such as software-defined perimeter technology and augmented intelligence paired with some of the most secure and modern data center assets in the world.

Shira Rubinoff: There are many different types of cyberwarfare that the U.S. can face, such as weaponized ransomware, **distributed denial-of-service (DDoS)** attacks, and outages, among others. Is there one avenue of attack that stands out the most as being the most threatening, and if so, why?

Brigadier General Gregory Touhill: Before I focus on the avenues of attack, I'll go back to some of the fundamentals. When we started talking about cyberwarfare and even before we used the term "cyber" (it was "information warfare" or "information operations"), we were focusing on the core tenets of what has now been called "cybersecurity": maintaining the confidentiality, the integrity, and the availability of information.

Early on, we saw things like **denial-of-service (DoS)** attacks tackling availability and basically denying information from people. We've seen hacking, such as what we had in Target and OPM, and some of the other "ripped-from-the-headlines" breaches, which were attacks that breached confidentiality of information.

I think looking forward, the most pernicious attacks are going to be based on the integrity of information, where people are going to use a host of different capabilities to go in and tamper with information, not unlike ransomware. The difference is that with traditional ransomware you say, "Hey, I'm going to scramble it up and then I'll give you the key for a certain amount of money."

With information being at risk as it is, I view an attack on the integrity of information using more than one tool as perhaps the most pernicious attack vector that we're going to be seeing in the near future.

Shira Rubinoff: Are there any stories that you could share about different types of cyberwarfare that you were involved in?

Brigadier General Gregory Touhill: I shouldn't disclose the identity of the victims yet, but what I can do is talk more about the tactics, techniques, and procedures that we observed with some of the adversaries, and then some of the lessons learned from those incidents.

While you can say that "if only the victim had done this, the incident would have been preventable," you can also take a look at it through the lens of "the victim could have raised the cost for the attacker so that the attack was made unappealing."

When I was working with the U.S. Government, we had incidents that started with a phishing attack. One of the things that we saw in both the public and private sector was a total lack of leveraging the tools that were available.

When it came to phishing, we knew that capabilities such as **Domain-based Message Authentication, Reporting, and Conformance** (**DMARC**), **Sender Policy Framework** (**SPF**), and **DomainKeys Identified Mail** (**DKIM**) were available, which would help to reduce our risk of exposure to phishing, by often doing a better job of authenticating sources and so on. Yet across public sector organizations, and government agencies and departments, as well as a lot of private sector entities (in fact most private sector entities that we responded to in our incident response), we found a lack of DMARC, SPF, and DKIM in place. It was disturbing.

Adversaries know this information because they look and see what kind of capabilities their targets have. They'll normally just go with regular phishing, as opposed to necessarily spear phishing. The really sophisticated actors, who know what they are looking for, are going to do their homework.

That brings up another point—people tend to put out a whole bunch of juicy and valuable information on the Internet.

As a cyber operator, if I was trying to do something malicious, the first place I would start looking for information is out on the Internet. I'm going to use search engines such as Google to go and do my reconnaissance. I'm going to go on LinkedIn as well.

Shira Rubinoff: Would you say that social media is a really big vector for gathering information to utilize in cyberwarfare? There's obviously the huge amount of information that people are currently putting out there because of oversharing. Do you find that to be a big problem?

Brigadier General Gregory Touhill: Absolutely. Let me give you an example. I met with a company that is a huge retailer and it asked me to come in and help to educate the workforce on why they need to be thinking ahead about security.

I basically was asked to show how I would attack them. What I ended up doing was starting on the Internet and spending about an hour putting together an attack. I briefed the group of about 300 or 350 engineers and I said, "Okay, I'm going come in and I'm going to attack you."

I knew that as a retailer, the company was trying to go into the cloud and the Internet commerce realm. It was going to try and learn as much as possible about doing online transactions and getting a cloud presence. In fact, the company was already putting that information out on the Internet as one of its strategic goals.

I went over to LinkedIn and I just drilled down through the LinkedIn profiles of employees until I found the cloud architects. Then I found the guy who was identified as being absolutely crucial to the company's pivot into the cloud. I thought, "This guy seems to be a critical node in the strategy; how can I influence him so that I can interrupt the path into the cloud?" I was thinking as an attacker.

I went to his LinkedIn page, where I learned a lot about him. Next, I went over to Facebook and I learned more. I found out how many kids he had and where he lived. I actually got a realtor interactive walking tour of his house online, so I knew everything about the inside of his house.

I found out where his kids went to school, then I worked out where his kids went for activities after school because, by the way, this was all posted on the Internet. I knew that his kids, when they left school, walked to the local YMCA to go to swim team. It was truly evil, but if I was an adversary and I had wanted to interrupt or sabotage him, that would have been possible.

By using assets that were freely available on the Internet and social media platforms, this key engineer was identified to me by his own company online. He was key to the company's strategy for the next decade, yet I was able to find out everything about this guy. If I was truly nefarious, I could have conducted a cyber operation combined with basic criminal activity. I could have intimidated that individual and perhaps compromised the company's pivot to Internet commerce. I may even have had the ability to coerce that guy into sabotaging the company's goals.

That example had a really positive impact from the standpoint of helping the engineers to wake up and smell the coffee. The truth is that similar activities are being done every day. Social engineering remains a great threat and we still need to train people.

There are some of my colleagues who think that everything needs to be automated and if we automate everything, we'll be able to defend against everything. I don't agree with that. I've found that people still have to program and code. I can go along with some of my other cyber operator colleagues and we can figure out a way to defeat most technologies out there, given enough time. If you can't defeat the technologies, you can always go on to defeat the people.

Another example is if you take a look at Equifax. The House Oversight Committee did a report on Equifax and the Struts vulnerability. A lot of people have been hot and bothered by the fact that the reporting indicates that the Equifax people did not properly patch and configure critical vulnerabilities in the Apache Struts software, and they should be. Equifax should have been on top of that, but it's a much more complex issue than that in my view because there are so many different critical vulnerabilities that come out on a daily basis.

I think from a public standpoint, the takeaway is to patch the critical vulnerabilities as soon as you can and if you can't patch them right away, implement compensating controls, which could range from taking the vulnerable application or device offline to constantly standing on guard staring at the app or device to ensure nobody exploits the vulnerability. There are lots of different things you can do with compensating controls.

Shira Rubinoff: We have many companies saying that the reason they don't update and don't patch is that there are far too many patches out there. How do they stay on top of the latest and greatest without being overwhelmed? Any helpful hints?

Brigadier General Gregory Touhill: I think we are going to have many pivots here in the next ten years. The Apache Struts vulnerability that was cited in the Equifax breach was just one of a litany of vulnerabilities in Struts that have been out for years.

I came into the Department of Homeland Security in 2014 and shortly after I arrived, we had an Apache Struts vulnerability. In the aftermath of the Equifax breach, everybody was getting target fixation on that one particular vulnerability, and I think it's really important that you do patch when you find that you've got a critical vulnerability. However, what's lost in the conversation is: why do we continue to put out software that continues to have a bunch of vulnerabilities, and why aren't we following secure coding standards? Why are the products as bad as they appear to be?

I don't think that that's a conversation that's toward the top of people's agendas. In my classrooms at Carnegie Mellon University, and as the President of Cyxtera Group talking with my clients, I'm asked questions like these now: "Why are some of these things that are coming out always requiring patches? Are manufacturers putting out a product with known deficiencies with plans to fix it after it gains market share (a pre-planned product improvement approach)? Is that part of the strategy?"

Frankly, I can't speak for a lot of the manufacturers that are out there, but I think that we need to be very discerning customers. We need to be asking those questions. I think that's going to be something that is part of the very public conversation.

As we see GDPR and some other regulatory regimes coming in, maybe we're going to see some consumer product protections and the penalties will be higher for companies that are not putting out quality products.

Shira Rubinoff: What are your thoughts around quantum computing as it becomes a reality, with the prospect of it being able to hack into any computer system in the world within seconds? How can we protect against it?

Brigadier General Gregory Touhill: Quantum computing is a fascinating concept. It's still aspirational, as opposed to operational, at this point, but research that is being done points towards some really fantastic capabilities.

I know the Army Research Lab here in the U.S. has been working with several top-drawer universities. In Australia, I believe that the University of New South Wales is doing some great stuff. The Chinese have assembled an impressive array of scholars, many of whom were educated here in the U.S. The Chinese have been doing some very interesting and sometimes alarming research into different applications for quantum computing. But I think at this point, there's still a long way to go before quantum computing goes into an operational mode.

Programming for quantum computing is something that I know many of the researchers are still trying to scratch the itch on, but that said, once they crack the nut, it's going to be a game changer.

I've always said that you can't have privacy without security and you can't have security without privacy. I'm concerned that with quantum computing and with some of the promises that are being made, we risk kissing the area of security and the age of privacy goodbye. I'm keeping an eye on it and I think that the jury is still out as to what all of the implications are, but from a privacy and a security standpoint, if everything pans out as some of the theorists are saying it will, we're going to have to rethink many different things.

Shira Rubinoff: If everything is interconnected, would a solution to maybe solving some of these quantum computing problems be to disconnect?

Brigadier General Gregory Touhill: Yes, we may decide to disconnect things. When I was the A6 for Allied Air Forces in the Middle East, we made a decision when we were building the Radio over IP network, providing support to the convoys, that as part of our security construct, we were going to go with private networking. We weren't going to connect at all. There are examples where maybe it's better not to connect, and frankly, as I went through evaluations of government systems, I'd often ask, "Why do you have to have this connected to the Internet?"

Shira Rubinoff: Earlier we discussed oversharing. Even if a system isn't interconnected, would you agree that there are still human vulnerabilities involved and mistakes that can happen?

Brigadier General Gregory Touhill: Yes. There is the debate over the idea that humans can't keep up, so we just need to use artificial intelligence and the like to manage all of this. I find that disturbing; I don't agree with that. We do need to have smarter machines, but we also need to have smarter people.

I'm a huge proponent of training and education, and there is a difference between the two. I define training as teaching someone how to do something, whereas education teaches why that is needed. If you don't combine training and education together, and people don't know why they should be doing something, they'll never do it right. Training and education are critically important as we do our day-to-day business, as well as when we look to the future.

In short, as we take a look at better ways to protect national prosperity and national security, we have to recognize that our economy, our societal institutions, and our day-to-day life has now become reliant on information technology. No place on earth has as much risk exposure as the U.S.

When we are taking a look at some new technologies, such as artificial intelligence or quantum computing, more and more people want to automate more and connect to the Internet. We need to make sure that from an ethics standpoint, from a security standpoint, from a policy standpoint, and from a technology standpoint that we know what the worst-case scenario is. With the IoT, for example, we all should be asking, "Why do we need this?

Does this improve our lives? Does this improve security?" Just because you can, it doesn't mean you should.

Shira Rubinoff: The speed of the world today, as you're saying, needs to be questioned. For companies too, speed is a factor to get ahead because if you're not online, you're not relevant. If you're not relevant, you're not in the game, so the idea is to just get online and fix any problems later. I think that's become the Achilles' heel in some of these problems. Besides the training, awareness, and education, do you have any other advice for companies?

Brigadier General Gregory Touhill: I believe that security itself can be a driver of business. As I go around and talk to boards and C-suites, I'm starting to see that some companies are, in fact, marketing their security capabilities as a reason why clients should come to them as opposed to their competitors.

In the past, security organizations were viewed as cost centers and there are now many companies making the pivot to being drivers of business. If more and more organizations on the commercial side looked at security as an enabling function that drives value and can be marketed as such, I think that we would actually see an acceleration of capabilities that would better protect national prosperity and national security everywhere.

Shira Rubinoff: You've talked in the past about people and companies moving to Zero Trust. Can you share a little bit about that and why you believe in it?

Brigadier General Gregory Touhill: I became very passionate about Zero Trust strategy shortly after I heard about it a couple of years ago. It was actually coined by John Kindervag back in 2006, while he was over at Forrester.

People continue to rely on the **Transmission Control Protocol/ Internet Protocol (TCP/IP)**, which was built in the '70s, an era when everybody knew each other, so they just wanted to make things work; they wanted to be able to communicate from point A to point B. You would connect and then you would authenticate after that. That's how everything is put together now.

As a cyber operator, I learned that we could leverage those weaknesses in TCP/IP to do our bidding. There were incidents including the Edward Snowden betrayal, Private Manning, and some stunning third-party defeats, such as what we saw with OPM. A third-party contractor to the Office of Personnel Management was breached by an adversary, who leveraged a compromised username and password, gained control of the third-party network, and then surfed in looking and acting like a legitimate user, using a trusted connection between OPM and the third-party contractor's network. For me, that was the last straw. I realized that having a Zero Trust strategy is essential if we're going to protect our assets.

Zero Trust basically means that every engagement needs to be authenticated before you connect. Furthermore, the thing that I really like about software-defined perimeter technologies, such as what we have at Cyxtera with the AppGate product, is that when you connect, after the authentication, you should only connect to what you're authorized to see.

I'm trying to educate and inform boards, C-suites, and my clients as to why it's important to have a Zero Trust strategy and how to implement it, so that they are more effective, efficient, and secure. I'm passionate about it because frankly, I've seen up close the impacts of not adopting a Zero Trust strategy and the terrible effects that it can have.

OPM alone included over a billion dollars in damages. How did I figure that out? Well, OPM was committed to doing 100 million dollars a year of identity protections for the victims who subscribed for that. That was a billion-dollar expenditure that the Federal Government was committed to because of that breach.

If you add up all of the different breaches, and all of the different incidents that could have been prevented by implementing a Zero Trust strategy properly, I think we could have saved arguably hundreds of billions of dollars a year every year, not only in the public sector, but also the private sector.

Shira Rubinoff: How do you explain what Zero Trust means to a company in simple terms?

Brigadier General Gregory Touhill: In essence, from a strategic standpoint, you want to make sure that instead of connecting and then authenticating, every engagement is authenticated.

Instead of just trusting that Gary on the other side of the connection is Gary, you're asking for an identity-centric approach to verify the link. What you can do with some capabilities that are out there is leverage things like **multi-factor authentication** (**MFA**)—at least two factors of control to make sure that it is, in fact, Gary.

If Gary is coming in to access some information that is, let's say, on-premises—it's in one of your facilities, or it could be in a data center, or wherever you have that information—before Gary can get in, you're going to ascertain a couple of things: first of all, is it Gary? Is Gary on a properly configured device? You don't want to have Gary coming in off a device that's in an unknown Starbucks, or for him to have borrowed a laptop if you don't know where it's been. You want to make sure that it's actually Gary, he's on a proper type of device, and there is a secure connection.

A lot of people talk about **virtual private networks** (**VPNs**) as the acme of secure connections. I think that's bad because VPNs have now become like cholesterol in arteries—they are clogging up firewalls. Firewall administrators are swamped managing firewall rules for each and every VPN. For example, in the DoD, we have some systems that have close to 100,000 firewall rules, and most are associated with VPN management! VPNs also drill a hole right through your defenses, neutering your intrusion detection and intrusion protection systems. It is time to retire this 23-year-old technology and upgrade to software-defined perimeters.

If you take a look at software-defined perimeters, they are built in with a secure connection. So now Gary is going to come in, knock on the door, and say, "Hi, it's Gary. I'm here to access this information." The software-defined perimeter technology is going to use the existing MFA, and reply, "Prove that you're really Gary." It's going to challenge Gary for something he knows, but also with something he has, such as an MFA token or third-party type of thing.

Gary's device is going to be checked to make sure he's got the proper antivirus in place and it's properly configured to meet security requirements. After Gary has been identified and his role determined, he will be let in. However, everything is securely encrypted so that Gary is only going in to the areas that he is authorized for. The rest of the network and all the other stuff that he's not authorized to go into, he doesn't even see.

Rather than Gary just coming in off the computer that he usually comes in on, or at least a computer that appears to be the same computer, or just using a technique like a username and password that's easily defeated or shared by careless people, we're going to use secure modern tools that are currently available to reduce complexity for our operators while increasing our defensive capabilities against our foes.

That's important in today's environment because cyber criminals and nation state actors like to masquerade as somebody else. They're going to try to come in looking like Gary, then they're going to get into your network and elevate privileges, for example, getting onto a machine and pivoting out of Gary's role to gain system administrator privileges. That's what we call elevating privileges.

Next, that attacker is going to move laterally—they're going to try spreading out across the network, taking total control of your network, and then pilfering it or using it as a launch pad for attacking somebody else, or a whole host of different things.

Zero Trust reduces your attack surface. Bad actors want to gain control of their target and the means to doing that is usually gaining control of the entire network. Moreover, when they gain control of your network, they can use your network as a potential launching pad for an attack on somebody else. Instead of having all your information hanging out there to be exploited, the Zero Trust approach reduces your attack surface down to a pinprick. The available information is only what Gary is authorized to see. You can use controls that say, "If Gary's only supposed to be working between set hours, that's the only time he's getting in." This adds granularity and better control over your information. I think that we need to better protect our country, our businesses, and our privacy.

Shira Rubinoff: Earlier we touched upon the Snowden situation. As we all know, Snowden was an American computer professional, former CIA employee, and former contractor for the U.S. Government who copied and leaked classified information from the NSA in 2013. His disclosure revealed numerous global surveillance programs run by the NSA and Five Eyes. What would you like to share about that? How could it have been prevented and what were the lessons learned around that?

Brigadier General Gregory Touhill: I am very passionate about this situation. First of all, I do not believe that Snowden was heroic whatsoever. There are many people who think that he was a hero for what he did, but I don't think so.

Anybody who aggregates information under a folder called "stuff to steal" has malicious intent. I think the Snowden episode, for all its criminal activities, should serve as a wake-up call not only in the public sector, but in the private sector as well. Once again, this is a reason why I came to embrace Zero Trust—I haven't run into a single organization that has not embraced the use of third-party contractors to provide the necessary highly skilled capabilities.

The days of having a homogeneous organization, where everybody was part of the same organization and had 100% loyalty to the organization, are now just a pipe dream. You don't know whether everybody is sharing the same loyalty as the person at the top or the person at the bottom.

As you take a look at how you want to organize and secure your information, you have to realize that you may have some people who aren't even members of your organization and have been brought in as third-party contractors, system administrators, and so on who may have privileges to information without you realizing. Snowden certainly had access to a lot of information that he shouldn't have. The facts clearly support that there were breaches in procedures, such as people sharing passwords and usernames. There was a lack of MFA in some areas that should have been corrected, and was not in time.

At the end of the day, what if you do have a turncoat in your organization like Snowden? How much risk are you willing to accept? If Zero Trust is your security strategy, as I think it should be, how can you better use the technologies that are out there, such as software-defined perimeters, to better protect your brand, your reputation, your mission, and the vital information that you're the custodian of? I think that Snowden is a watershed example of why we need to embrace Zero Trust, particularly in today's environment where we rely so heavily on third-party so-called experts to help us in all of our missions.

Shira Rubinoff: In all your interactions with companies, and the talks that you give, what is the reception you get when you talk about Zero Trust? Are more people now understanding that Zero Trust is a must-have?

Brigadier General Gregory Touhill: I get a mixed reaction. Overwhelmingly, with the boards and the C-suites, they get it. They agree from a strategy standpoint that they need to do it.

However, some of the organizational inertia comes not at that C-suite and board level but at the middle management level. Part of that is because that layer of the organization is often task-saturated and really hasn't had the time to keep up with some of the latest technologies. Middle management is often sent on wild-goose chases with eager executives who chase fads and not the latest capabilities.

When I speak to middle management people, who are the people who actually have to implement the strategies, the demonstrations are really compelling for them—being able to show them how they could reduce their overhead, or being able to retire VPNs in favor of a software-defined perimeter. Once they see it, they are hooked and they're able to see how they can easily implement a Zero Trust strategy with some technologies that DARPA kick started back in the early part of the 21st century.

Playing catch-up is difficult because there are some essential activities that people have neglected. For example, if you go into most organizations, I'll bet they have been extremely lazy or lax in making sure that their Active Directory is up-to-date, and by that, I mean that the data that's entered into Active Directory is relevant, timely, and accurate.

If you want to go and do role-based access control, for example, you need to have something like Active Directory in place, where you can actually link with MFA and other capabilities to have an identity-centric approach.

In summary, generally the people at the top get it, while the middle management people want to see it first, but once they see it working, they become believers.

We need to make sure that we invest in training and education for everybody up and down the chain of command to take a look at things from a holistic standpoint. We've got many people who are resistant to change, but for all the wrong reasons.

The way we're doing business right now, along with the way we're attacking cybersecurity and protecting our information, is not tenable for the future. We can't continue doing the same things that we're doing now and expect the results to get any better. We're going to need to have people go out there and retire ancient and antique technologies. We're going to have to do things smarter and better to free up the workforce to focus on the tasks that they can't get done now. I think that's fair.

Shira Rubinoff: Thank you, Brigadier General Gregory Touhill.

Discussion

The General's fascinating career as a trailblazer in an increasingly cyber-driven world gives us some clear takeaways, about how the changing nature of threats and global cyberwarfare should drive your security posture and cyber hygiene. Technology often solves old problems while creating new ones, and cybersecurity has to evolve to meet these ever-changing challenges. The General underscores several topics that are relevant to your security posture, including the pivotal nature of human factors, social media as a weapon, and how increased connectivity is sometimes regressive for security.

In the not so distant past, we tended to compartmentalize the way we viewed technological progress, because we didn't have a more holistic view of the spillover effects of technology. Society functioned in a much more linear fashion, with technology being simplistic and specifically earmarked to assist with menial tasks.

We didn't view technology in an integrated sense, because it hadn't reached the level of sophistication or maturity needed to become embedded in every step of the workflow and in the augmentation of workforce performance. Fast forward to today, and technology is omnipresent. Warfare is no exception.

Preventing cyberattacks

Prevention is easier said than done. In an age of convenience, systems that are universal have seen a proliferation of access points. Naturally, the very nature of modern computing, with its plethora of access points, can end up being your cybersecurity Achilles' heel.

Despite the supremacy of computing, managing human factors in cybersecurity remains a formidable task that can limit the efficacy of your defenses. The General's take on Edward Snowden, whose theft of information was splashed across every newspaper globally, is a prime example of how human factors need to be the centerpiece of your security posture.

If you peel back the layers of the Snowden case, it's straightforward; a classic malicious insider threat attack. It played out like this: a trusted source within the organization had access to all data within the organization. From that starting point, Snowden had free reign over all data across the organization. He was able to lift that data in order to make an internationally received political message.

Thinking critically about the Snowden case casts light on the reality of modern times. The security of the past cannot be the security of today, since as technology becomes more sophisticated, the methods of attack mature as well. Cyberwars are raging, and to be prepared for the inevitable tests of your security posture, you have to think macro and micro and create an iron-clad protocol for people, processes, and technology.

In the end, the process is what secures everything. Naturally, the devil is in the details of the process, because how the interactions between people and technology are managed is often the ultimate determinant of your success or failure.

Zero Trust

Going back to Snowden, the General highlights this as a classic reason as to why Zero Trust needs to be implemented across all organizations. Access needs to be granted only on a case-by-case basis, with appropriate identity credentials for every move across the organization.

Zero Trust would have prevented this situation from occurring, and averted this crime. Snowden stole the information on a USB, but in a Zero Trust environment, he wouldn't have been able to download any sensitive data onto it. Never mind that he snuck through security with a USB; that information wouldn't have been accessible to him in the first place.

Social media

Social media has been adopted as a part of modern life for several years now, and its near-universal adoption by people all over the world has allowed it to become a battleground for cyberwarfare. Oversharing is rife, and parameters for what ought to be considered appropriate behavior on social media is very far from defined.

It's not surprising that people often blur the lines between their personal and professional social media presence. Once people leave their work environment, they use their personal social media liberally. The mindset is that this is how I communicate; this is how I share my life with my family and friends, and I have the right to live openly online. The problem is that this can quickly become a major issue that calls your entire cybersecurity posture into question.

The General highlighted this common problem with his LinkedIn example, but it's applicable to many social platforms. The process is as follows: when somebody's looking to penetrate an organization, they can create a profile that has similar attributes and demographics to the person they're targeting, creating a level of familiarity, which in turn creates trust. Bad actors can create discussions with their target around affinities such as hobbies, education, geography, and a number of other key demographic information that helps them gain traction.

What begins as a low-level conversation around something appealing to the targets can escalate quickly. Eventually, in true social media fashion, the target will often overshare key details of themselves, enabling the attacker to mimic that targeted person, thereby gaining access to systems easily. Employees at all levels of your organization should be educated on this phenomenon, and recognize the tell-tale signs of the weaponization of social media to pull off cyber heists.

Disconnection – how progress can be regressive

Through the General's decorated military service, we see how progress is often regressive when it comes to cybersecurity. In an age of ever-increasing connectedness, it's often the right move to disconnect systems from the Internet. Thinking about military systems, it's straightforward that a successful cyber incursion could have devastating consequences; there are non-military systems that are equally essential, for which disconnection should be seriously considered.

The General's experience in the Middle East also illuminates that connection to the Internet shouldn't be the default. In many instances, there is no compelling case to make that a connection is actually needed. This idea is especially relevant amid the slow move toward quantum computing.

Nevertheless, disconnection from the Internet doesn't make systems hack-proof. It's important to recognize that there are still human vulnerabilities and mistakes that can cause holes in security even when systems aren't connected to the Internet. Humans are humans, and mistakes can happen even with an isolated system.

Summary

As cyberwarfare becomes increasingly prevalent with time, the need to develop powerful defenses grows. Furthermore, because attackers sometimes target businesses, organizations, and individuals—either as their ultimate targets or in order to assemble large networks of "zombies" for use in attacking government entities—the growing need for powerful defenses impacts everyone, not just people working for government agencies. As the General mentioned, "The way we're doing business right now, along with the way we're attacking cybersecurity and protecting our information, is not tenable for the future."

9

Can Artificial Intelligence (AI) be Trusted to Run Cybersecurity?

Preparing for the onslaught of the ongoing cyberwars means you need to leverage the best available technology, to keep your organization safe. But can we trust these technologies when it comes to running our cybersecurity?

Artificial intelligence (**AI**) refers to the ability of computers to learn in ways similar to the ways that humans learn—providing machines with the ability to act with wisdom even in unfamiliar situations. The applications of AI include machine learning, knowledge reasoning, planning, robotics, **natural language processing** (**NLP**), computer vision, and artificial general intelligence.

There's little doubt that AI will play a larger and larger rule role in human society as time progresses, and its role in the realm of cybersecurity is already a hot topic of discussion among strategic thinkers in the field.

One area of debate, for example, is whether or not humans will ever be able to trust AI to run cybersecurity by itself. Many subject matter experts seem to believe that, if AI is implemented correctly, not only will it be trustworthy, but it may deliver greatly improved security.

Today, the majority of cybersecurity technologies utilize some sort of signature- or rule-based engine that requires heavy human involvement. These cybersecurity systems require continuous updates to their "rules"—a need that is not only incredibly time-consuming from an employee perspective, but also causes employees to be unable to get a full global look at the enterprise; rather, it limits them to analyzing a single part at a time. As such, AI is a game changer when it comes to time-sensitive tasks and will reduce error percentages when compared to humans.

At least in the near term, the role of the human will always be an integral part of cybersecurity, but we will soon see that role coupled with the utilization of AI that truly trains systems to mimic human intelligence via continuous learning. AI can analyze immense amounts of data rapidly, looking for outliers, as well as drive the rapid detection of cyber incidents and automated responses. Care has to be taken in the development of AI for these systems, so as to not trigger bias-based AI, which can be prevalent in at least three areas: the data utilized by the program itself, the people who design these systems, and the designers of the associated datasets from which the system learns.

The element of human bias in designing these systems is a hotly debated topic in the cyber/AI world. Typically, the population designing these systems has been pulled from a non-diverse group—similar in age, race, gender, and so on—creating a biased look at how AI views systems, which in turn does not provide the best security for an enterprise. A truly diverse population needs to be tapped to develop the designs, as well as the data and the program itself.

According to the **World Economic Forum (WEF)**, systems must be able to account for globally diversified perspectives, and there needs to be a distributed intelligence network that can adjust to new data, incorporate new models of thinking, and benefit from cultural diversity. The WEF further suggests that if we flip the current model to be built up from data rather than imposing data upon it, then we can develop an evidence-based, idea-rich approach to building scalable AI systems—resulting in delivering insights and understanding beyond those that we can achieve with our current modes of thinking.

Another advantage to such a bottom-up approach, the WEF explains, is that the system could be much more flexible and reactive. It could adapt as data changes and new perspectives are incorporated. Consider the system as a scaffold of incremental insights so that, should any piece prove inadequate, the entire system does not fail. We could also account for much more diversified input from around the globe, developing iterative signals to achieve cumulative models, to which AI can respond.

We're still seeing just the very beginning of how AI can impact cybersecurity and assist in creating far greater cybersecure environments.

I had the pleasure of interviewing two top voices in the AI space, Mark Lynd and Joseph Steinberg. Each comes from a strong security background with deep knowledge and insight into the world of AI. Mark Lynd has served as a CIO for over two decades and, today, does various expert and influencer work in the cybersecurity and AI fields. Joseph Steinberg, who previously invented several popular cybersecurity technologies, is today one of the most-read columnists covering cybersecurity and emerging technologies and their impact on the human experience.

In this chapter we'll travel from the core of how AI is defined and understood, to the state of applications, cybersecurity, and AI integration; from where we are today, to what we can expect in the next couple of years, and beyond.

Mark Lynd (CISSP, ISSAP, ISSMP) is a top-ranked global consultant, speaker, and practitioner for cybersecurity, AI, and IoT. He has been an accomplished C-level innovator, technologist, board member, and global thought leader for more than 20 years. Mark has served as a CIO, CTO and CISO, adviser, consultant, and thought leader for several large enterprises.

Mark was named an Ernst & Young's "Entrepreneur of Year – Southwest Region" Finalist, presented the Doak Walker Award on ESPN's CFB Awards Show to a national television audience, and has been featured/quoted in the Wall Street Journal, InformationWeek, eWeek, CRN, CSO, and others.

Mark holds a Bachelor of Science from the University of Tulsa, and honorably served in the U.S. Army in the 3rd Ranger Battalion and 82nd Airborne.

Shira Rubinoff: A lot of people lump together AI and machine learning, thinking that they are one and the same, not really understanding the differences between them. Are you able to give a quick description of what each one is and how they're different, and whether they should be utilized hand-in-hand or not?

Mark Lynd: Machine learning is a subset of AI. AI has genetic algorithms, expert systems, machine learning, deep learning, and so on. There are even some areas that people argue should be in there that aren't. Conversely, there are some areas that are in there that really shouldn't be.

The reality is that over the years, especially through the '90s and the '00s, there was a real focus on expert systems and there was some neural network stuff going on, but it struggled.

In the mid-'00s, neural networks started to take off. People were beginning to put more resources behind them, and they started to have enough data to effectively train the models.

When you look at this field just from the different levels of abstraction, you have AI at the top level and machine learning is underneath. Deep learning is actually a subset of machine learning. Machine learning is a subset of AI that focuses on systems that can learn from data, identify patterns, and make automated decisions with minimal human interaction, but it is still a subset of AI just like deep learning.

Shira Rubinoff: Is using AI the best way to solve some of our strategic problems? How does that relate to cybersecurity?

Mark Lynd: Yes, I think so. It's mainly about the use cases within the AI arena. AI is the big buzzword now, so there's lots of hype.

When you choose AI to try to solve some of the bigger strategic problems around data, and also around cybersecurity, it's often because you're trying to solve some of the simpler challenges early on, and then move up to things that might have a greater impact. That way, you understand what your data looks like and if you're going to be able to detect problems or identify threats. If you're using AI for cybersecurity and you try to bite off everything at one time, then it's probably too much.

Using AI to identify patterns that humans can't and identify threats is really important. There's also a really strong use case for AI in cybersecurity specifically in the form of machine learning or deep learning. Making sure that your data has the security information that you're going to be able to use with AI is a critical first step in that process.

By solving a simpler problem first, you get the ability to start to do some interesting things. The data will define how far you can take AI and how many use cases—especially around cybersecurity within an enterprise—you'll be able to tackle.

Shira Rubinoff: Do many organizations have the data that's needed to be successful when implementing AI?

Mark Lynd: I think many companies do have the data; they just don't know where all that data is, or whether it is usable.

It takes a lot of data to properly train a model. It's not just historical data that's important, but also future collections and current streams of data when you're trying to effectively use AI.

Unfortunately, there is bias in data and there are things in data that can cause problems, which can negatively affect your outcomes. When you look at data from an AI model perspective, you need to use large amounts of data to learn. When you're learning, more data and better data will allow specific algorithms to assist the model in learning more successfully. The more that the model is able to learn, the better tuning you're going to get and the greater precision you're going to have. Also it's going to reduce the potentially negative effect that noise may have on the model.

There are many opinions on this, but I think most people would say that large amounts of high-quality data are absolutely critical and required for driving good AI use cases.

Shira Rubinoff: Is our existing technology environment and infrastructure capable of supporting AI? If so, can you please explain that? If not, what's needed to actually pull that together to make it possible to support AI?

Mark Lynd: I think most environments today are hybrid environments: they have some cloud and they also have on-premise. This might be geographically dispersed, both inside and outside the perimeter, or the perimeter might be extended into the cloud so that you have a larger environment, which from a cybersecurity perspective obviously creates its own challenges.

AI is really good at looking at data derived from perimeter devices and software, but you need to collect all that data. For all of these monitoring products, SIM, SIEM products, and other products, you're pulling in log files, SNMP, and syslog. You're pulling in all this information to give you an idea of whether the infrastructure can handle it and secure it, or if there are anomalies or issues occurring.

I think most people are now starting to expand their horizons around using the cloud more effectively. All the big companies—IBM Watson, Microsoft, and Google—are offering these cloud services to extend and augment your current environment if you have really large datasets, or if your algorithms require a great deal of CPU. Making investments on-premise is not what it used to be, and most people are really pushing hybrid environments, especially if they're streaming data in or pulling real-time data in. Having that ability to dynamically expand your footprint is very difficult on-premise, but that's what the cloud was built for.

Shira Rubinoff: You mentioned bias earlier. Do organizations truly understand the ethical and bias issues when considering AI, and what would those be? Do they understand the repercussions of any such biases on cybersecurity?

Mark Lynd: Yes, interestingly, in cybersecurity and AI many people think of machine learning, algorithms, and so on, but one of the issues that's receiving more attention now is ethics in AI. These are things like racial, geographical, and ethnic biases in systems. It is important that these issues are getting more attention now, given their potential effects on the cybersecurity outcomes derived from AI.

We're still in the early days of identifying how to root out this bias and ensure that we have a way to gauge it, and monitor it on an ongoing basis. People like Elon Musk and the late Stephen Hawking came out and talked about the potential sinister outcomes that AI could have, if it's allowed to go unfettered. But I think what most people in enterprises are more worried about is the broader topic of the distribution of wealth. Will greater use of AI by a few people cause greater disparity in the distribution of wealth? People are worried about that; you see that fear in elections in many countries.

There is racial, geographical, and ethnic bias in applications, and it's crept into AI for sure. Humans are coding the algorithms. We're collecting the data, and the data may have bias in it as well. So, we need to make sure that we have safeguards when testing and that there's compliance around that.

I think the other important point is, as we interact with more AI systems, does it actually blur the line between behavior and outcomes? There is a difference. What unintended outcome will arise and then how will we adjust to that? How will we make sure that we're able to respond and remain compliant? How will we make sure we're providing a system that's actually trying to drive toward the outcome that we desire, and isn't affected by the different types of bias that may creep into the system and into an organization?

Fortunately, most organizations are treating these AI systems as part of IT projects and not in the broader sense, so there's compliance and oversight. If this doesn't happen, there's a mismatch in the goals, and the projects don't get the care and love that they need to try to root out any bias in the system. Sometimes projects end up not going toward what the original outcome or desire was.

Shira Rubinoff: Something I speak about regularly is diversity of thought and mind. Obviously, people code a certain way in order to yield the outcome they want in the technology. Do you have any pointers or suggestions in order to circumvent the bias?

Mark Lynd: The first thing is to acknowledge that there's the potential for bias, and then, during your testing period especially, you should see if you can identify or determine that there's bias in the system, and what impact it's having on the overall outcome.

Ask, "Is this compliant with what the company stands for and what the brand stands for? Does it affect customer information? Does this make us more secure?" Those type of things should be considered. It's important to have oversight of that.

So many AI projects are high-visibility because there's a lot of money being put into them. They need people who are outside of IT to be on board; they just can't be from within IT. I think that's a real mistake that companies have made in the past, and many of them have learned from it.

We've started to see some CISOs and CSOs move outside of IT. We're also beginning to see that with AI in projects and steering committees.

Whatever a company uses for their oversight and compliance, they have other people that are in the business take part, instead of solely IT being involved in the delivery of the project. People outside of IT can often more effectively determine whether a project's compliant with what the company stands for, or whether it's how the company wants to be represented. Does the project violate any relationships with customers, or customer data? That process should happen early on as part of the testing.

Also, I think good code reviews of the algorithms are needed to make sure that there's no bias. Screening the data is best practice for AI projects.

Shira Rubinoff: Does an organization need to have a strategic plan to utilize, monitor, and evaluate AI?

Mark Lynd: Yes, I think it's really important to have a strategic plan. If you don't have a strategic plan, you don't understand how AI potentially affects the other things that you're doing.

AI uses data that's collected from other applications or other systems. If you have a strategic plan, you know where you're getting this data from and you've decided to add these new streams of data. What effect is that going to have and is that data something you can use in other AI projects, or an extension of an existing AI project, to get better outcomes? This could help to support growth in the business, reduce costs, or drive efficiency.

AI, especially machine learning and deep learning, is driven by large amounts of data. If you think strategically and you collect the data in such a way that it can be easily grouped into areas, like a data lake, where AI can access the data and run it, I think there are some really amazing outcomes and some potential future AI projects, or extensions of current projects, that really could do great things for businesses.

Everybody in these businesses can almost think, "If we could use AI, we could be more efficient, or we could provide better information, or better services, or products to our customers." Having the data and having a strategic plan to collect and use that data, along with prioritizing your AI projects and then deploying them, is really critical. That requires planning and a thoughtful approach from not just IT, but also from the business.

A strategic plan is fundamentally critical, especially as more companies become digital. We hear about digital transformation constantly, and that has an impact on cybersecurity, because if you're becoming more digital, you're more susceptible to cyber threats.

If you have a strategic plan, security should be part of it early on. If it's an AI project, I think that might be important because that project has access to all the data. A strategic plan helps you to put everything together, look at your resources, refine what it is you're trying to do, and make sure that you're compliant, so the best outcomes can be achieved.

Shira Rubinoff: Thank you, Mark Lynd.

To extend our conversation on AI and cybersecurity, I've paired Joseph Steinberg's interview with Mark's. He'll help us explore the past, present, and future of this technology, while homing in on the human factors that heavily influence AI from inception to deployment.

Joseph Steinberg

Joseph Steinberg is one of the most-read columnists in the cybersecurity field and a respected authority on other emerging technologies, having amassed millions of readers as a regular columnist for *Forbes* and *Inc.* magazines. Within three months of going independent in April 2018, his column—now published exclusively on `JosephSteinberg.com`—reached 1 million monthly views. His writing reflects his passion for exploring the impact of emerging technologies on human society, making complex technical concepts simple to understand, and helping people focus on the technology issues and cybersecurity risks that truly impact them.

Joseph previously led businesses and divisions within the information security industry for more than two decades, has been calculated to be one of the top three cybersecurity influencers worldwide, and has written popular books ranging from *Cybersecurity For Dummies* to the official study guide from which many Chief Information Security Officers (CISOs) study for their certification exams.

Joseph is also one of only 28 people worldwide to hold the full suite of advanced information security certifications (CISSP, ISSAP, ISSMP, and CSSLP), indicating that he possesses a rare, robust knowledge of information security that is both broad and deep; his information security-related inventions are cited in more than 400 U.S. patent filings.

In addition to his writing, Joseph advises businesses in the cybersecurity and emerging technologies sectors, helping them grow and succeed. He also serves as an expert witness and consultant on related matters.

Joseph can be reached at `https://JosephSteinberg.com`.

Shira Rubinoff: Could you start by discussing your background?

Joseph Steinberg: I've been in the information security space since the commercialization of the Internet in the mid-1990s, which, considering how much technology has advanced in the last 25 years, might as well be the Jurassic era when it comes to information security and Internet technology.

I've had many different roles over the years. I started on the technical side in engineering roles, and moved up the ladder. I ultimately ran several departments at a cybersecurity product vendor, before founding my own companies to bring to market several information security technologies that I invented.

Ultimately, I ended up moving into the advisory space. For about 20 years I've been writing various articles about information security. About seven years ago, I joined *Forbes* as a contributor covering information security, never expecting my column to become a significant element of my career. When *Forbes* left New York, and my editor moved on, I moved my column to *Inc.* magazine, and expanded it to cover emerging technologies. Last year, in 2018, I took my column independent. Readership skyrocketed, to the point that within three months of going independent I was getting about a million reads per month.

Today, I spend about half of my time writing articles related to information security, emerging technologies, and their impacts on human society. I don't typically relay news, but, rather, provide insights and give readers food for thought about important topics. The other half of my time I spend helping companies as an advisor. In some cases, I help firms in areas related to cybersecurity, and, in others, I work with cybersecurity and other technology companies themselves—helping them establish their reputations, build strategic relationships, and succeed in general.

I've also written several books on information security ranging from *Cybersecurity For Dummies* for non-technical people, to the official study guide from which CISOs study for certification exams.

Shira Rubinoff: How do you feel that AI is impacting cybersecurity?

Joseph Steinberg: First and foremost, it's important to understand that the AI revolution is not delivering simply another incremental technological advancement—it is totally overhauling the world as we know it.

In the same way that the Industrial Revolution replaced human muscles with machines that were much stronger, faster, and more reliable, AI is replacing human brains with computer minds that will also eventually be orders of magnitude smarter, faster, and more reliable than even the smartest people.

Consider how much faster a modern laptop computer can accurately solve complex math problems than a human being can, and now imagine that type of cognitive difference when it comes to every other form of thinking—including, eventually, social types of learning. With that in mind, it's easy to understand why every area of life for humans is going to be changed by AI.

When we talk specifically about cybersecurity in relation to AI, there're two primary areas that we need to address.

Firstly, we need to recognize that deploying AI in every aspect of human life will increase cybersecurity risks—and likely create some dangers that could have tremendous ramifications for civilization as a whole.

Secondly, we must consider the elements of AI that can be used for cybersecurity-related purposes, from both offensive and defensive perspectives.

Those are really two separate conversations, even though they're clearly both tied to the growing influence of AI in our world.

Shira Rubinoff: When it comes to AI, there's the human element needed to get it running. Do you perceive human involvement as being a detriment to AI when it comes to cybersecurity?

Joseph Steinberg: As you mentioned, for our current, early generations of AI systems to work well, the AI systems' development must include people with AI expertise and people with domain expertise. So, today, for example, if you're creating an AI system related to cybersecurity, you definitely need cybersecurity experts involved in the process.

While the definition of AI seems to change with time, when it comes to what's typically called AI today, we are talking about systems that learn—meaning systems that can make decisions about situations that they've never encountered before, based on previous circumstances and situations from which they have extrapolated various rules, that they can then apply.

As such, one area of AI system development that typically requires the human involvement of those with domain expertise is ensuring that any dataset provided to the AI (from which it is supposed to learn) is robust enough for the AI to actually learn what it needs to learn.

If an AI system is developed without adequately feeding in appropriate data, the results that it generates in the future may be deficient. We have seen this occur several times with various forms of computer systems. For example, a facial recognition system that was created by light-skinned people, and which was fed primarily images of light-skinned people for its initial dataset, had difficulty recognizing dark-skinned people.

The deficiencies in that system did not result from racism, but, rather, because the developers had primarily light skin themselves, and used images of themselves as sample data while testing, not realizing that the dataset was inadequately robust; in fact, once a more robust dataset was introduced, it was discovered that tweaks also had to be made to the system in order for it to properly learn how to do its job with the full range of possible values to which it would be exposed in the future.

The need to ensure that adequate data is supplied to the AI applies in the case of cybersecurity as well. Occurrences that may be anomalous and indicative of problems in one environment may not be so in another environment. If you're creating a general anomaly-detection cybersecurity engine with AI, for example, you'd need to make sure that the data going in as examples of normal usage represent system usage that's totally free from anything problematic, and that the dataset covers sufficiently diverse situations, from which the AI can adequately learn about any potential problems that may occur down the line. If you don't provide enough data from which to learn—the AI will not be capable of finding some relevant anomalies, and, if something goes undetected, you could have a serious cybersecurity problem on your hands. Of course, you don't know what every possible future scenario looks like—that's why you want AI on your side in the first place—but, if the AI has not learned enough, it will not be able to properly handle scenarios that you want it to address. Likewise, if the AI is learning while in production, you need to make sure that the humans handling cybersecurity incidents do so properly (that is, they need cybersecurity domain expertise)—as the AI will be learning from their reactions to specific conditions how to address similar scenarios, if they occur in the future.

Another issue vis-à-vis AI and humans is the human bias that can be introduced as a result of human involvement. While morals and values may vary between societies, most people have morals and values that they consider important that, at times, they let override statistical probability.

Let me give you an example from the security world. Imagine that three people about whom you know nothing show up at the same airport counter to buy plane tickets for the same flight, and that you are the cashier, armed with an AI system that's supposed to predict the risk level that a particular person may pose to the plane and its passengers.

One person approaching the gate was born in Salt Lake City, and has spent, as far as you can tell, his whole life there. The second person was born in New York City and has spent her whole life there. The final person was born in Iraq. There is a possibility that the AI, using statistical analysis, will assign a greater level of risk to the person from Iraq, based on nothing else other than the location at which the individual was born—which is, of course, something that the person did not even choose and may provide absolutely no real-world indication of risk.

As a society, we find the idea of subjecting a person to extra security checks based on such prejudice to be generally repulsive, despite the relevant statistical probabilities. We believe that we should not judge people based on things that are beyond their control and that do not indicate anything about their individual values or behaviors. But an AI system that works by learning the patterns of past terrorist attacks may find that no known terrorists were born in Salt Lake City, and that no female terrorists were born and have lived their entire lives in New York, but that many known terrorists were born in Iraq—and it may weigh such information as it evaluates the risk that a potential passenger poses. When coupled with the other factors—which may be identical for all three passengers—it may produce a risk score that is higher for the person from Iraq than for the other two individuals.

The conflict between accurate learning and values that we hold dear is not a simple one to resolve—when do we tell an AI that although it correctly statistically predicted something, we don't want it to use that information because it is "wrong" to do so? In fact, AI, to a certain extent, is the ultimate example of prejudice—automating the process of learning from past experiences how to handle future situations, even when new people are involved.

Shira Rubinoff: There are some schools of thought that say that you need diverse rulesets because otherwise, you'll have different types of learnings based on a certain gender, for example. Do you agree with that?

Joseph Steinberg: As I said before, you need a robust dataset. And that dataset must have the right diversity. You, for example, mentioned gender. For certain systems, gender is going to be important—and if you do not have proper gender diversity the AI will make bad predictions. However, if you are creating an AI system that makes predictions related to prostate cancer, for example, gender diversity is not going to be a major factor in determining how well the system works; the inclusion of males of different ethnicities, of various age groups, from diverse geographic locations, and so on will be much more relevant.

Domain expertise is important for determining what you need in a dataset in order to get the right results, and in what ways the dataset must be diverse; guessing is almost always going to produce bad results.

Shira Rubinoff: There's also a big worry around whether AI can be commandeered and misused for all sorts of attacks. What would you say on that point?

Joseph Steinberg: Some smart people have predicted that AI could spell the end of humanity. I'm not that pessimistic, but I do recognize that there are some tremendous risks, and that we absolutely must make dramatic improvements in cybersecurity in order to prevent various catastrophes from occurring.

As an example of a risk that already exists, consider that just recently some researchers from Israel demonstrated an AI-type system that learned what various cancers look like on a **magnetic resonance imaging (MRI)** scan and what healthy scans lacking cancer look like. The AI was then able to manipulate the MRI scans of people with cancer to remove the cancer, and to take scans from people without cancer and add it in.

The AI did such a good job at changing the images, that even after the researchers involved told radiologists who were reviewing the altered scans that some of the scans had been modified by AI, the radiologists could not identify which ones showed real cancer and which had bogus cancer added, and could not distinguish between scans from healthy people and those from people with cancer whose cancer was digitally "removed." In fact, even though the group of experienced radiologists had a different AI helping them, they still made wrong decisions in more than half of the cases.

As a result of the research it's clear that if you do not adequately protect all components of the MRI process—the scanning machines themselves, the network to which they're attached, the infrastructure involved, the software controlling the devices and managing the data, the disks and/or files containing the images—with some sort of mechanism to prevent manipulation, you could have an absolute disaster on your hands. People could literally commit murder. They could use an AI to remove cancer on a person's scans, causing the person to suffer and die as the cancer remains untreated. An evildoer could also cause unnecessary surgeries by causing doctors to see cancer on scans when no cancer was actually present. And MRIs are just the tip of the iceberg.

The point is that AI systems are going to be doing more and more things. Today we do have drones, but they're not making decisions all on their own. Someday, however, they might. Let's say that someone was able to take control of an AI-enabled drone or feed it bad data, and thereby transform a friendly bomber into an enemy bomber. There are lots of things that can go wrong the minute you rely on autonomous and automated learning, especially if anyone can manipulate the datasets going in.

The other thing to keep in mind is that unlike a bug in a system that produces a bad result, in the case of bad data, you may never realize that the AI was making bad decisions until it is far too late.

Datasets sometimes contain millions or billions of records. If somebody inserted a few valid, but untrue, records into that dataset, or manipulated some records, how would anyone go about finding the problem after the fact?

In short—we simply cannot afford, in a world of ubiquitous AIs, to have the kind of breaches that we have now. For AI to work, and for it to work safely, major improvements will be needed in terms of cybersecurity.

Shira Rubinoff: What would improving cybersecurity look like?

Joseph Steinberg: It would involve shoring up the security around everything that's using AI, and protecting other systems from the dangers that AIs create. In the case of the MRI systems that I mentioned before, for example, there are specific areas in which obvious improvements can help. Today, images are typically not stored or transmitted with encryption. There is no hash or digital signature created on each image, so one cannot easily verify that an image has not been modified. There are no proper access controls to the image-reading systems either, and few hospital terminals have proper physical security controls.

These and other soft points that open the door for AI dangers have to be addressed. Today, computer systems in a bank are often better protected than systems in a hospital. If we protect money, we should be protecting human lives—and we must act before AI dramatically increases the risk to the latter.

Another area of concern vis-à-vis AI and cybersecurity is that as an offensive mechanism, criminals could use an AI that's designed to try to find vulnerabilities and launch attacks. They could also attack by feeding bad data into AI systems, thereby manipulating their performance—often in ways that cannot easily be detected ex post facto.

Essentially, AI is going to make the challenge of cybersecurity much greater by increasing the stakes. The damage will be a lot worse than today if something goes wrong. It's hard to imagine the full scope of that right now.

Shira Rubinoff: On a personal basis, do you have any real-world stories you could share?

Joseph Steinberg: Of course. As I mentioned previously, the definition of AI seems to be a moving target. Less than a decade ago, when we started talking to AIs such as Alex a and Siri, such interactions were cited as examples of using AI. Facial recognition technology was also typically classified as AI.

Several years ago, someone sued Apple after he was arrested because someone had stolen his ID and used it in an Apple shop, which led to Apple technologically associating the innocent person with the criminal. From that point, things spun out of control. Police ultimately figured out that the person who was apprehended was not the same person as had been in the Apple store.

If AI's going to be used for facial recognition in the future, it needs to be made smarter so that it can quickly realize that a thief using a stolen ID is not the person whose details appear on the ID.

Shira Rubinoff: There are those who worry that AI and automation will take away jobs. Do you agree?

Joseph Steinberg: Obviously, AI will have an impact on human jobs as it matures. Centuries down the road, if we continue improving technology at the rate that we are today, it's conceivable that AI will be able to do every possible job much better than humans ever could, creating a situation in which no humans are needed to do any work. How society will adjust as it transitions to that point will definitely be a challenge, and major sociological issues will have to be addressed.

In the shorter term, we will also see major societal impacts. We are not that far away from a time in which there could potentially be no human truck drivers on American highways. That thought may sound crazy today, but we are likely much closer to the day that such a scenario becomes reality than many people realize. The potential gains for trucking companies of migrating to self-driving vehicles are dramatic—trucks wouldn't have to stop for eight hours at night in order to sleep, and they wouldn't have to stop moving in order go to the bathroom or to eat. As such, self-driving trucks would offer efficiency gains per vehicle of somewhere around 50% upfront, while simultaneously reducing the cost of shipping by eliminating the need to pay a driver.

What happens to all of the truck drivers as AI takes over American shipping? What happens to all of the rest stops and all of the restaurants that truckers support? There will obviously be jobs lost, and significant societal changes, certainly at the beginning.

Such changes will be painful, but people will progress to other jobs—and, the reality is that regardless of whether the changes are "good" or "bad" they are going to happen, so we might as well prepare accordingly.

There were zero jobs in cybersecurity 100 years ago. There were zero jobs programming personal computers and networks 100 years ago. As technologies improve, there'll be many new jobs created as well. We must stop teaching people for the past, and start training them for the jobs of the future. That said, if AI does progress as it potentially could, we'll have to look at things like universal income and how we support a society in which the vast majority of people may not need to, or be able to, compete with AI workers.

Shira Rubinoff: What do you see as being the future for AI in cybersecurity?

Joseph Steinberg: When it comes to cybersecurity, we can already see things happening both from a defensive position and from an offensive position.

From the defensive position, one of the greatest challenges that organizations face today in cybersecurity is that they've invested in many great products, but they cannot deal with the tremendous volume of alerts that those products create.

Thankfully, the vast majority of alerts do not represent situations or events that are urgent, but sometimes identifying which alerts need to be addressed ASAP is like finding a needle in a haystack—or worse. One of the roles that AI is playing right now from a defensive perspective is learning about networks, user behavior, and what goes on within the technology ecosystem of an organization. Based on that, the AI can help security teams decide which alerts are most critical, and how to prioritize tasks.

Today, we're not yet at the stage at which organizations will let AI address a major cybersecurity problem on its own without human intervention. But we'll get to that point—probably a lot sooner than many people might imagine, at least for certain types of cybersecurity issues.

On the flip side, from an attack perspective, AI can be used to help create and enhance strategies, techniques, and technologies used for attacking others.

It can, for example, learn by analyzing the results of numerous attacks, and then help criminals decide which cyberweapons to use in which environments. It may also help criminals select targets, not only based on the chances of achieving a successful breach, but also based on whether the AI estimates that the target's defenses are likely to lead to the perpetrator getting caught.

Another way in which AI poses a risk to cyber defenders is that it can help attackers undermine authentication—which is a serious problem that, for some reason, is not receiving sufficient media attention.

Take the case of biometrics and voiceprints, for example. When you place a phone call to any one of the numerous banks using such technology today, the bank authenticates you not only by checking that you know the correct password for your account, but also by listening to your voice and comparing it to previously known recordings (some financial institutions even use voiceprint on its own to authenticate users—with no need for anyone whose voiceprint has already been recorded to enter a password). While voiceprint technology has greatly improved over time, and voiceprint authentication has become well accepted industrywide, AI might undermine its potency. How hard would it be for a properly designed and coded AI to simulate somebody's voice quite accurately if it were given significant amounts of recordings from which to learn?

Likewise, how hard would it be for an AI to deceive a facial recognition system by creating a "deepfake" type video to display to a camera when the system prompts "the user" to stand in front of it? We don't yet know the answer to this question, but, it seems clear that as time goes on, we're going to see exactly such a mechanism utilized to trick authentication systems.

In short, the battle between human attackers and human defenders is evolving into one in which both sides are equipped with all sorts of AI technology. If they are not doing so already, criminals will use AI to get around all sorts of authentication mechanisms, and to improve other forms of cyber attacks. Eventually, however, as AI technology improves, AIs may even create other AIs that fill the roles that today are staffed by humans. Cybersecurity may eventually become a nearly human-less profession—as AIs battle against one another for supremacy.

Shira Rubinoff: Thank you, Joseph Steinberg.

Discussion

As we learned from both these experts, the AI revolution isn't just the newest technology; integration of AI into our processes is already changing the world as we know it. Similar to the industrial revolution, when we replaced human muscle with machines that yield much stronger and faster work outcomes, AI is and will be replacing human minds with computers that will eventually produce more nimble and reliable outcomes from data. These outcomes and accompanying analysis will be more accurate and precise than the most brilliant minds of our time. Simply put, AI is a game changer for the human experience, and will augment our bandwidth and capabilities as workers and regular citizens.

AI can get rid of menial tasks and bolster your cybersecurity. It will also broaden your organizational ability to swallow and analyze large amounts of information, and subsequently give meaningful results much faster than it would take for a human to get to solutions. AI equals greater efficiency, but this doesn't mean AI is the panacea for all of the persistent challenges within your organization. Yes, we can safely say that you can mostly wave goodbye to menial tasks that may bedevil people at your company, but there are pitfalls that you should be aware of when paving the path toward full integration of AI into your daily operations.

Joseph and Mark provided us with an excellent overview of the intersection between AI and cybersecurity. Specifically, I'd like to revisit (1) The importance of a strategic plan for your AI integration, (2) How bias is transmitted through computing and what you can do to prevent it, and (3) The destructive potential of AI that can alter the course of human history.

The importance of a strategic plan for your AI integration

Through these interviews, we learned that efficiency can equal better security or the need for less security, depending on how you choose to integrate AI into your organization. Given that deploying the same technology can lead to wildly divergent outcomes, Mark emphasizes the critical need for an organization to have a strategic plan to utilize, monitor, and evaluate AI, to ensure proper cyber hygiene.

Without a clear strategic trajectory, you won't understand how AI could potentially affect other parts of your organization. If you can't clearly delineate the impact of AI on your present infrastructure, you could be creating gaping holes in your security posture without being aware that you've created a weak point.

As mentioned, if done right, AI integration is a win-win for everyone. The proper implementation of AI can help you grow a business, ensure accuracy, and, in turn, reduce costs, eliminate repetitive tasks, drive efficiency, and improve your cybersecurity posture. If done wrong, it will create new potential gaps in your cyber defensive strategy, as mentioned in the interviews.

To successfully integrate AI with proper cyber hygiene, knowing your data, a topic that I've covered extensively in this book, is absolutely essential. To be truly acquainted with your data, you need to know what it is, where it sits, and what relevant regulations dictate the storage of the data. Additionally, you must be armed with information about the data that's collected from other applications and systems. Knowing your data helps you to determine your strategic plan, which, in turn, can help you to identify how to merge data with other streams of data throughout the integration of AI.

This clear demarcation of where we deploy and use AI, as Joseph explains, will help us to laser focus on areas where there are actually increasing cybersecurity risks. Naturally, the integration of new technology will create dangers that can have risks and ramifications for your organization. Knowing the origins of those potential pain points can make all the difference.

AI isn't just about obviating menial tasks, as it can surely be leveraged to improve your cyber defenses. When it comes to securing an environment or an organization or technology that's being implemented, utilizing AI with cybersecurity can and will make our solutions and proactive security processes that much more nimble. This can keep us ahead of the game, instead of being mostly reactive to the situations that land on our laps, which has been the case until very recently.

AI is changing the cybersecurity landscape, but the same rules of cybersecurity apply: it's important that we're proactive and reactive in our strategic plan to stay ahead of our adversaries and their rapidly evolving methods of wreaking havoc.

It's imperative to have a formalized process through a strategic plan that leverages AI to improve security. After all, many of our potential adversaries lean on the same sort of AI-driven technology to cause us harm.

How bias is transmitted through computing and what you can do to prevent it

Human bias, whether conscious or unconscious, persistently seeps into computing through a variety of ways. It's not hard to figure out why: humans are biased, and as they program computers, their worldview and biases are often hardwired into the programs that organizations use to drive their businesses every day.

As Mark mentions, one of the issues in AI that's receiving massive attention is the great concern over ethics and how racial, geographic, and gender bias can cause great harm. AI and cybersecurity are both relevant to this phenomenon as mitigating these biases is imperative to maintaining your cyber hygiene and preventing damage to your bottom line. It's important that these issues get more attention given the potential cybersecurity outcomes from AI.

The light-skin biases in many of today's most popular technologies are a straightforward example of how bias is already seeping into our systems and heavily affecting outcomes. The developers who tested their technology may have mostly light skin. For convenience purposes, they probably used themselves as sample data while doing this testing without realizing their data set was inadequate and focused on a very specific subset of a population (much of the world's population has darker skin than these developers). Eventually, consumers who don't fit in this demographic find out that their technology has failed them when their darker skin becomes a barrier to their gadget working properly. The recent "Gender Shades" study by MIT researchers Joy Buolamwini and Timnit Gebru substantiated this phenomenon, and details how a lack of diversity in development failed darker-skinned users.

Thinking about AI along the same lines, it will always be biased if we don't pull data from a diverse population. One of the things we have to be careful about is the process of how the inputs, especially in terms of whoever is coding for AI, make their way into the system, and remain acutely aware of the potential human bias that can creep into the system. We have to constantly assess our work with the following question—was it coded in a biased way that could skew the results and forever taint our work processes?

Consider how this applies to cybersecurity, as diversity of people also yields diversity of thought and mind. If you have a staff that better represents the world, you'll create a more secure environment. This is because the knowledge and wealth of viewpoints allow your team to attack the problem from different angles, so your security will benefit from these varied backgrounds.

To bolster the efficacy of your operators and your cyber hygiene and prevent devastating outcomes, we need to ensure that adequate, appropriate, and unbiased data is supplied when programming with and for AI, as Joseph explained. When talking about accuracy in collecting data and mitigating unconscious bias, it's also important to focus on domain expertise for each area you are managing.

You need to determine what you need for each data set to be integral and accurate. Ask yourself the questions: (1) What do the data sets mean? (2) What is their purpose? (3) What are the potential pitfalls that may skew your system? Know your data in order to determine what these data sets need to include to be wholeheartedly inclusive. Each piece of all the data sets must reflect these goals in order to skirt by unconscious and conscious biases. If you are vigilant against bias, you'll emerge with an organization that's more nimble, effective, and efficient, and has impeccable cyber hygiene.

The destructive potential of AI that can alter the course of human history

With great strides forward in AI, major global predicaments for humanity may arise. As organizations increase their capacity to carry out their day-to-day operations more effectively and efficiently, so too will the capacity of bad actors to inflict unimaginable harm on anyone they target increase.

We saw, through the case in Israel mentioned by Joseph, how AI could be used for nefarious purposes that are beyond many people's imaginations. A simple visit to the doctor by an important politician could be turned into a political crisis that destabilizes an entire democracy.

Joseph walked through just one simulation that's enough to scare anyone about the prospect of AI going forward. Let's say a presidential candidate goes for a routine medical visit and, based on AI knowledge, a bug or virus is put into the results that mimics stage 4 cancer in an MRI.

This could cause the candidate to pull out of the race. As this is a national political candidate, this malfeasance would have a global effect; one attack vector could potentially change history.

Walking through the same simulation on the flip side, a person visiting the doctor for an ordinary well-being checkup has cancer, but the system is manipulated based on AI knowledge and the image showing the growth is altered, resulting in this person being given a clean bill of health.

This could potentially result in the death of this patient, who is woefully unaware of the dire health situation that they're currently facing. The example illustrates how AI in the wrong hands can create devastating consequences for nearly any organization, government, or person, by altering outcomes.

Naturally, the adaptation of new technology carries significant risks. There is a wealth of literature and cinema dedicated to dystopian futures where machines take over humanity. The prospects of AI are so brilliant that we have to worry about how the power of this technology is going to be used by evildoers.

Takeaways

We have to stop and think about the enormous impact that AI will have on our way of life going forward. The course of human civilization will be fundamentally altered as we integrate AI into every aspect of our daily life, including cybersecurity.

From a cybersecurity angle, we live in a world where we have to expect the worst. Never let your guard down, and protect every entrance to your system. Also, think critically about different perspectives and how AI, when not managed properly or protected, can be subverted and radically alter results. If you can imagine it, someone has probably already imagined that same scenario as well.

The good news is that with proper cyber hygiene you can prevent horrific incursions that cause massive destruction. As I've stated in past chapters, knowing your data, being acquainted with and cognizant of potential threats, and being hyper focused on your proactive and reactive security posture will allow you to put your best foot forward and save yourself from an acute cyber crisis.

10 Conclusion

We're only starting to see the importance that cybersecurity plays in our organizations and daily lives. Through expert interviews and focused commentary, I've highlighted what I wholeheartedly believe lies at the crux of the challenges that we're currently experiencing or will be dealing with in the not-so-distant future, and that's making sure you have the right processes in place to integrate the humans and security technology in your business.

We delved deeply into the challenges that are quickly evolving and will threaten our ability to thrive in the near future, unless we're prepared and forward thinking in our cybersecurity mindset and actions. It's critical that the problems of tomorrow are factored into our present proactive and reactive security posture.

The way we perceive cybersecurity within organizations must evolve. While many organizations have made great strides in better integrating cybersecurity holistically, there is still a great deal of work to be done. Notably, boards all over the world are realizing the power of and the need for a cybersecurity presence on the board itself. This illustrates that cybersecurity is finally starting to be understood as an integral piece of an entire organization's daily operations.

We shouldn't be satisfied with the status quo. Despite the flurry of threats that they face, many organizations are still very limited in their vision when engaging in budgeting and planning for their fiscal year. They still view cybersecurity as a line item in a budget, to be minimized, when in reality cybersecurity ultimately secures their entire bottom line.

Cybersecurity should be approached as a critical need in an organization's process, including training, global awareness, updated security and patching, and instituting a Zero Trust model. These essential four steps to achieving proper cyber hygiene, which I've underscored throughout the book, should be implemented as standard in every single organization.

In addition to these steps, there are many emerging facets of cybersecurity that must be analyzed and reviewed; as we've discovered, technology advances rapidly, and the cybersecurity landscape will continue to change substantially with every passing year.

Continuous training

Adding the organizational diversity that your company needs means that in the future, your cybersecurity needs will be tailored to meet a variety of challenges. The exact processes you'll need will be dictated by your organization's particular inner workings, business model, or what they do on a day-to-day basis; but the one thing you must keep in mind is that without a process to effectively deliver ongoing training to a diverse company, your training will become stale, routine, and ultimately ineffective.

Taking into account that your organization has both a proactive and reactive security posture, we know that what worked yesterday cannot be counted on to work tomorrow. We must put processes in place to regularly update our proactive posture against modern threats, and test our reactive capacity to limit harm from new technologies.

Culture of awareness

As well as individual organizations building an internal culture of cybersecurity, the industry as a whole is beginning to comprehend the power of working together toward common solutions. Accordingly, large organizations are increasingly banding together to share intel across the cybersecurity sphere. They're doing this with the understanding that we're all stronger as a collective unit, rather than standing alone in dealing with the bad actors that are moving at lightning pace to infiltrate our organizations.

It's important for your organization to put processes in place to extend your security-aware culture beyond the bounds of your own employees and workflows, and engage effectively with other organizations in the same industry to mutually improve your cybersecurity.

Up-to-date security

As we've discussed, sometimes cybersecurity professionals glaze over the basics and run out-of-date, unsupported OSs as a matter of convenience. This is a common phenomenon because many organizations are already large and spread out or are growing so rapidly that those in charge have trouble keeping track of every single device. It's not always easy, but running an updated OS is essential. Having the right, forward-looking processes in place to identify the next necessary update and prepare for it as far ahead of time as possible is essential. Bad actors keep their technology up to date and wait eagerly for the next update; your organization needs to be just as eager for the next opportunity to add to their security.

Patching is a task that can be cumbersome, expensive, and time consuming. That's why it's critical for an organization to have the right process—a designated group of people that handle patching. This key group of professionals need the power to decide when and how patching needs to occur, and they'll need the right tools and support from the organization to get the job done while minimizing impacts to day-to-day operations.

Zero Trust

Zero Trust dictates that organizations should not give automatic access to anything inside or outside of its perimeters that requests access. Instead, every attempt to access data needs to be verifiable before access is granted. Zero Trust means zero access until that entity can be properly authorized, and this policy extends to machines, IP addresses, and the like.

Zero Trust also creates additional steps, whereby someone who got access to certain area doesn't suddenly have free reign over all of your data. In the past, if a bad actor successfully made it inside your perimeter, they became trusted and further access would be granted.

In the same way, people inside of organizations who had access to a particular subset of data, automatically had access all of the data, even if it wasn't appropriate for their line of work. Instead, Zero Trust limits access to data appropriately.

Instituting Zero Trust is undeniably effective, if it's made as easy as possible for people. Adding these steps to verify identity makes things a tiny bit more inconvenient for the user, slowing them down by the smallest fraction, and as we've discussed, busy people reach for convenience over security far too often. Make sure you link Zero Trust to your training processes, so your employees know how vital it is; and make sure that there's a process in your proactive and reactive security posture to hunt for workarounds and backdoors, as well as being transparent about how these violations of Zero Trust are handled. Without the right process and culture, Zero Trust can be seen as just another burden to carry, but if your employees understand and embrace it, it becomes a vital cog in the cybersecurity machine.

Conclusion

Over the course of developing this book, it became clear how cybersecurity is impacting us every day, and touches many facets of our lives. As I reviewed each chapter, the specific technology or concept was heavily highlighted, but we always came back to the same conclusions about human factors. That's why the interplay of human factors within cybersecurity needs to be taken just as seriously as the technology itself.

Through the book, I've talked about how humans have historically been viewed as the weakest link in the security chain of an organization. I've highlighted the importance of making employees within your organization an integral part of the solution. Instead of viewing people as the problem, you can empower everyone in your organization to be solution.

In the end, your success will hinge on how you frame the people, process, and technology that I've laid out throughout the book. Specifically, organizations must understand the critical role that the process plays, as it acts as the glue between people and technology.

Cybersecurity needs to be viewed more globally and holistically within organizations; compliance culture is no longer relevant or effective. Today's threats call for a security culture, embedded in every single job at every single level, from the board all the way down to the interns. Dealing with humans at one level, technology at another level, and ignoring the processes that facilitate these interactions will undermine all of the efforts you make on either front.

Without focusing on the process, you'll derail your efforts to achieve complete security. An organization needs to succeed in melding these three essential elements of people, process, and technology if they're going to succeed in keeping cyber safe. Only then can you truly tackle the monumental challenges that will inevitably arise in the not-so-distant future.

Other Books You May Enjoy

If you enjoyed this book, you may be interested in this book by Packt:

Dancing with Qubits

Robert S. Sutor

ISBN: 978-1-83882-736-6

- See how quantum computing works, delve into the math behind it, what makes it different, and why it is so powerful with this quantum computing textbook
- Discover the complex, mind-bending mechanics that underpin quantum systems

- Understand the necessary concepts behind classical and quantum computing
- Refresh and extend your grasp of essential mathematics, computing, and quantum theory
- Explore the main applications of quantum computing to the fields of scientific computing, AI, and elsewhere
- Examine a detailed overview of qubits, quantum circuits, and quantum algorithm

Python Machine Learning - Third Edition

Sebastian Raschka, Vahid Mirjalili

ISBN: 978-1-78995-575-0

- Master the frameworks, models, and techniques that enable machines to 'learn' from data
- Use scikit-learn for machine learning and TensorFlow for deep learning
- Apply machine learning to image classification, sentiment analysis, intelligent web applications, and more
- Build and train neural networks, GANs, and other models
- Discover best practices for evaluating and tuning models
- Predict continuous target outcomes using regression analysis
- Dig deeper into textual and social media data using sentiment analysis

Leave a review - let other readers know what you think

Please share your thoughts on this book with others by leaving a review on the site that you bought it from. If you purchased the book from Amazon, please leave us an honest review on this book's Amazon page. This is vital so that other potential readers can see and use your unbiased opinion to make purchasing decisions, we can understand what our customers think about our products, and our authors can see your feedback on the title that they have worked with Packt to create. It will only take a few minutes of your time, but is valuable to other potential customers, our authors, and Packt. Thank you!

Index

A

Adams, Cleve
- about 126
- apps permissions 136
- career 126
- cloud services 130
- corporate network, hacking 136
- Cyber breaches 131
- cybersecurity 137
- cybersecurity, evolution 127
- cybersecurity risks 135
- cybersecurity, top trends 126
- identity 132
- information, leakage 131, 132
- information security 128
- operations and security, working with 128, 129
- password authentication 134, 135
- secure authentication 133, 134
- security policy, for security networking 132
- work protocols 129, 130

AI integration
- strategic plan, importance 214, 215

artificial intelligence (AI)
- about 120, 159, 193
- destructive potential 217, 218

AT&T Alien Labs 124

B

bias
- transmitted, through computing 216, 217

blockchain
- about 65, 66
- future 66, 67
- practical uses 67
- technologies 68, 69

Bring Your Own Device (BYOD)
- about 37, 112
- career-focused websites 40
- human factors 41
- oversharing, example on Facebook 38, 39
- oversharing, prevention 38

C

Cloud Controls Matrix (CCM) 74

collaborative defenses 142

compliance culture
about 3, 4
versus security culture 3
cost of data breach
reference link 20
cultural change 165, 166
cyberattacks
preventing 188, 189
cyber hygiene
about 5, 140, 141
human factors 5
risks, recognizing 26
technical underpinning, transitioning 17
cyber mindfulness
practicing 42
cyber risks
training, within organization 108, 109
cybersecurity
about 85
challenges 139
continuous training 222
data 86
future, implementing 87
in cloud 85, 86
through interviews 42, 43
cyberwarfare
security posture 188

D

data breaches 107
Davidson, Mary Ann
about 100
career 100, 101
career advice 106
cloud security 103, 104
cyber hygiene, strengthening 105, 106
data breaches, mitigating 105
data breaches, security and technology 101
data leading, mishandling 103
hackers, dealing 102
naval officer, experience 101
denial-of-service (DoS) 174
disgruntled employees
about 23
threat, solving 24
distributed denial-of-service (DDoS) attack 174
Dobrauz-Saldapenna, Guenther
about 47
blockchain 53
blockchain, collaboration 51
blockchain future 50
blockchain, innovation 48, 49
blockchain, security 53
blockchain technology, with cybersecurity 49
blockchain, use cases 51-53
Domain-based Message Authentication, Reporting and Conformance (DMARC) 175
DomainKeys Identified Mail (DKIM) 175

E

Eaves, Sally
about 55
AI, within optimal cyber risk program 61
automation, overview 58, 59
blockchain projects 63
blockchain technology 56
blockchain technology, cyber risk challenges 57, 59
blockchain technology, cybersecurity 60
blockchain technology, financial services and supply chain 60
blockchain technology, implementing 57, 58
blockchain technology, security 61, 62
career 56
cutting-edge research 63
security, versus cybersecurity 62
employees training, human factors
audience, for training 8
employees training, human factors in cyber hygiene
audience, for training 6, 7
information dumps, versus incremental training 9
real life scenarios 11
training, difference between 8
universally applicable, versus situationally relevant 10
Equifax hack
reference link 18

G

global awareness and culture, human factors in cyber hygiene
demographic monoculture, pitfalls 13, 14
diversity, building 13
global world, communicating 15, 16
Global IoT collaboration 166, 167
Global Positioning System (GPS) 147

H

holistic cybersecurity 140
human factors
compliance culture, versus security culture 3
problem and solution 2, 3
human factors, in cyber hygiene
about 5
employees, training 6
global awareness and culture 11, 12
Humpton, Barbara
about 147
career 147
cybersecurity 154
cybersecurity, access control 151

cybersecurity, best practices 151, 152
cybersecurity, leadership challenges 153
cybersecurity, maintaining 150
data, accessing 149, 150
IoT 154, 155
IoT, best practices 152
IoT digitalization 148, 149
IoT revolution 152
Siemens, using IoT connectivity 148
technology, impact 153

I

interconnectivity
risks 139
Internet of Things (IoT) 2, 115, 116, 165, 169
IoT-specific risks 167
IoT training gap 166

J

Jackson, Kevin L.
about 73
cloud, security controls 76
cloud security, cost-effective of protecting data 74, 75
cloud security, critical aspect 73, 74
cybersecurity, controls 75
cybersecurity, enforcing 76
cybersecurity, implementing 76
cybersecurity, monitoring 76
Johnson, Ann
about 156
AI, impact for IoT devices 161
ATM environments 159
attack, from IoT device 158, 159
blog 156, 157
cybersecurity, dealing with IoT 157
DDoS attack 160
IoT devices, securing 162, 163
IoT devices, standard 160
IoT security 162
job, security 163
Microsoft career 156
vulnerability management 160

K

Kellermann, Tom
about 91
cyber bank heists 96
cybercrime investigations 95
data breaches 91, 92
data breaches, preventing 93
data breaches, privacy regulations impacting 94, 95
data breaches, risks 93, 94
data protection 97-99

L

Lynd, Mark
about 196
AI and machine, difference

between 196, 197
AI, implementing 198
AI, supporting 198, 199
AI, used for solving strategic problems 197
bias, in system 200, 201
bias, on cybersecurity 199, 200
strategic plan, to evaluate AI 201

M

magnetic resonance imaging (MRI) 208
malicious attacks
disgruntled employees 23
opportunistic employees 23
Meftah, Barmak
about 117
AT&T Cybersecurity 124
autonomous cars 119
career 117
cybersecurity 119-123
cybersecurity, embedding into companies 121, 122
digital transformation, within organization 122, 123
integration, automation 125
security risks, with IoT 118, 119
threat researchers, ecosystem 124

N

natural language processing (NLP) 193
negligent behaviors, non-malicious insiders
about 33
lost or stolen device, report failure 35
passwords, security 34, 35
recycled passwords, issue 33, 34
Wi-Fi, unsecured 36

O

oblivious, non-malicious insiders
about 30
privacy, maintaining 31
risks 32
sensitive information 31, 32
unattended computers 30
Open Threat Exchange (OTX) 124
operating system (OS) 18
opportunistic employees
about 23
threat, solving 23
OS systems
next-gen authentication 111-113
updating, for optimal patching 111-113

P

patterns and developments
global awareness 109-111

R

radio frequency identification (RFID) 133
reactive security
implementing 114
Reavis, Jim
about 78
cloud computing/cloud security 84
cloud computing, types 79
cybersecurity, in cloud technology 80
data security 80, 81
digital transformation, in cloud 84
General Data Protection Regulation (GDPR) 81, 82
information security project, working 78, 79
IT and cloud trends, future 82, 83
regressive
progress 190, 191

S

security
updating 223
security and efficiency 141, 142
security-aware culture 222
security culture
about 4
versus compliance culture 3
security, development and operations (SecDevOps) 20
Sender Policy Framework (SPF) 175
social media 37, 189, 190
Steinberg, Joseph
about 203
AI, future in Cybersecurity 212, 213
AI, impacting on cybersecurity 204, 205
AI, risks 208-211
AI systems 205-207
career 204
cybersecurity, improving 210
gender diversity 208
URL 203

T

technical underpinning, cyber hygiene
updated security and patching 17
Zero Trust model, implementing 21, 22
Touhill, Gregory
about 173
career 173, 174
cyberwarfare 174, 175
information gathering, from social media 176-178
patches 178
quantum computing 179

quantum computing, problems 180
security 181
Snowden 185
Zero Trust 181-187

U

updated security and patching, cyber hygiene
Cognizant C-Suite 19
cost of data breach 20
crisis, averting 18
proactive and reactive security posture, need for 19, 20
Zero Trust model, transitioning 21

V

virtual private networks (VPNs) 130, 183
vulnerability management 168

W

World Economic Forum (WEF) 194

Z

Zero Trust 169, 189, 223, 224
Zero Trust model
implementing, limit access to sensitive data 113, 114
Zero Trust model, cyber hygiene
malicious and non-malicious attacks 22, 24
social engineering 24-26
threats and attacks 22

Printed in Great Britain
by Amazon

59200751R00149